GARDENING TIME

ALPINES AND ROCK PLANTS

HOWARD DRURY

CENTRAL

Boxtree

First published in Great Britain in 1988 by Boxtree Limited

Copyright © Central Independent Television plc 1988

ISBN 1 85283 227 4

Photographs appear by permission of the City of Birmingham and the Royal Botanic Gardens, Edinburgh

Line drawings by Mei Lim
Designed by Groom and Pickerill
Typeset by York House Typographic
Printed in Italy by New Interlitho Spâ, Milan
for Boxtree Ltd
36 Tavistock Street
London
WC2E 7PB

CONTENTS

PREFACE

The Gardening Time programmes was started in 1972 as a weekly feature and since then has continued to be produced 52 weeks of the year.

The garden is situated in a Birmingham park in the suburb of Kings Heath. The first two presenters of the programme, Cyril Fletcher and the late Bob Price created from a piece of waste ground a superb garden of just over one-third of an acre which contained a rockery waterfall and pool, island beds, paved areas, a small vegetable garden, a small soft fruit garden and the typical 8×20 greenhouse.

In 1983, the City of Birmingham Parks and Amenities Department gave permission to extend the garden to 7 acres. Work began on a adjacent site and to date we have created over 1½ acres of new gardens with different styles of landscape. There is also an extended vegetable garden with organic and non-organic trial bed areas, a large herb garden, and trial beds for roses, dahlias, chrysanthemums and bedding plants – all propagated from three new greenhouses.

The four expert presenters of the Gardening Time programme are Arthur Billitt (fruit and vegetables), Jock Davidson (house plants), Geoff Amos (all-round gardening, especially bedding plants) and Howard Drury (alpines, conifers, heathers, shrubs) who is also the programme's Horticultural Adviser.

The programme spans the entire year and these accompanying books show how, by doing the right things at the right time, anybody can become a successful amateur gardener.

JOHN PULLEN
PRODUCER

8

INTRODUCTION

This book is designed for the home gardener who, as a result of visiting some of the famous large botanical rock gardens in this country, feels the urge to reproduce certain features, albeit on a more modest scale, or to experiment with some of the species on show. Broadly speaking, although it is easier to create a natural garden when working on a fairly large scale, space need not preclude an original and attractive display, for the same groundwork rules apply. Do not be daunted by difficult sites, either in aspect or soil type, as there are always some suitable alpines available – even if you only wish to cover a small paved area, there is a wide array of plant material and containers that may be used. Alpines, and rock plants provide a challenge to all gardeners from the complete novice to the enthusiast, and the rewards for hard work and patience are immeasurable.

HOWARD DRURY

As a handy cross-reference for calculating plant dimensions, planting depths and distances, etc., where mentioned in the text, the following list gives approximate metric equivalents to imperial measurements.

½ in	1 cm	18 in	45 cm
1 in	2.5 cm	20 in	50 cm
2 in	5 cm	24 in	60 cm
3 in	7.5 cm	30 in	75 cm
4 in	10 cm	36 in	90 cm
5 in	13 cm	4 ft	1.2 m
6 in	15 cm	5 ft	1.5 m
7 in	18 cm	6 ft	1.8 m
8 in	20 cm	7 ft	2.1 m
9 in	23 cm	8 ft	2.4 m
10 in	25 cm	9 ft	2.7 m
11 in	28 cm	10 ft	3 m
12 in	30 cm	12 ft	3.6 m
15 in	38 cm	15 ft	4.5 m

1. PLANT NAMES

All plants are provided with Latin names, which are both important and necessary. Many gardeners shun Latin plant names in preference for common, or local, names which can sometimes be very confusing and even lead to the selection of wrong plants. Few botanists bother to inform gardeners that many of the Latin names merely relate to the collector who found a particular plant, or that it describes the colour, form or shape of various parts of a plant. (See table opposite.)

Where plants have limited things in common they are grouped together as plant families. Take, for example, the family Ericaceae which comprises plants such as ericas, callunas and rhododendrons. Although the foliage of rhododendrons and ericas may seem very different, the arrangement of the ten anthers and ovaries, together with the fused petals, is identical, although the flowers of rhododendrons, for example, are much larger than ericas.

The Latin plant name is usually in two or three parts. The first gives us the genus, which groups together many plants of a family that have similar botanical features, such as the arrangement of leaves and flowers. Examples of genera are *Primula, Erica, Juniperus* and *Dianthus*, and it is helpful to think of these as an individual's surname.

The second Latin name is termed the species, roughly equivalent to a person's forename. Where plants have evolved within a genus and have retained individual characteristics, they are termed species; and just as in a human family various individual members possess slightly different features – hair and eye colour, etc. – so in the plant world the second name, and sometimes the third (the variety), very often describes these botanical features.

Unfortunately, to add a little confusion, some species in the wild will breed and give rise to slightly different forms with almost identical characteristics. *Cotoneaster microphyllus* measures 6 ft across as a mature specimen; *cochleatus* is identical but only 12 in high; and *congestus* is much smaller, rarely attaining 4 in, yet still identical in all other ways. In some instances these differences are termed varieties, such as *Chamaecyparis obtusa* var. *formosana* which has smaller leaves than *C. obtusa* itself.

Many plants, such as primulas, give rise to seedlings that are occasionally of outstanding merit and in some instances these have been selected in cultivation and given cultivar names which are written in single inverted commas. There are many selected cultivar forms of *Primula auricula, Primula pubescens* and *Primula sieboldii*, for example, where the cultivatar 'Geisha Girl' has attractive edged petals.

Names describing habit and shape of plant

horizontalis	flat spreading	*Juniperus horizontalis*
repens	prostrate, creeping	*Ranunculus repens*
contorta	twisted	*Corylus avellana* 'Contorta'

Names describing vigour and size of plant, flower or foliage

major	large	*Vinca major*
nana	small, dwarf	*Lavandula spicata* 'Nana'
obtusa	rounded	*Chamaecyparis obtusa*

Names describing leaf shape

palmatum	hand-like	*Acer palmatum*
dissectum	finely cut	*Acer palmatum* 'Dissectum'

Names describing colour of stems, leaves or flowers

alba	white	*Primula marginata alba*
rosea	pink	*Primula rosea*
carnea	red	*Erica carnea*

Names describing geographical location in the wild

alpina	of the Alps	*Dianthus alpinus*
japonica	of Japan	*Primula japonica*
orientalis	of the Orient	*Thuja orientalis*

Names describing the flower

grandiflora	large-flowered	*Magnolia grandiflora*
plena	double	*Primula alba plena*
polyantha	many-flowered	*Primula × polyantha*

2. ALPINES IN THE WILD

The growing of alpines is one of the most fascinating ways of bringing together plants from many areas of the world, which will provide a wealth of colour for any garden, small or large, and for almost any aspect. The range of plants offers simplicity for the novice, labour-saving possibilities for the time conscious, and, for the more serious, a never-ending challenge to encourage plants to survive and even flower in alien environments.

Clarence Elliott, the distinguished alpine nurseryman, claimed he could write more books about the plants he had killed than those he had grown. Alpines have survived, often in very hostile conditions, for many hundreds of years in the wild. By copying, as closely as is practical, the soil and climatic conditions in which the plants grow naturally, we should be able to establish many of the more common types without any difficulty; and indeed, this guideline is often used as a basis for some of the rarer species.

Where plants are being grown for the first time, it is good practice to obtain copies of the notes written by celebrated collectors such as Kingdom Wand, who introduced many gentians and primulas, and George Forrest, who gave his life collecting alpines in China. Successful growing of alpines depends on looking closely at their native conditions.

The term 'alpine' refers to a range of plants that are found between the eternal snow line, (the point high up on the mountain where the snow never melts) and the small shrubs and trees that are found growing lower down mountain sides. Alpines are found at altitudes as high as 19,000 ft (5,800 m) in certain mountain ranges, but as low as sea level in the Arctic zones. In the European Alps they are generally found above 4,500-6,000 ft (1,370-1,830 m), and in countries such as Switzerland and Italy they provide a blaze of colour on the upper slopes as the snow melts.

Many people bitten by the alpine bug visit areas such as these to see plants often growing in difficult and appalling conditions. The soil types vary greatly according to rock type and historical formation. Some plants are found in heavy clays, whilst most thrive on a well-drained, extremely gritty medium. Some have an almost continual supply of water, whilst others cling to rock faces and crevices, and are rarely soaked by rain or melting snow, a practice that can be copied in the rock garden by planting lewisias, haberleas and ramondas in vertical crevices. And yet other plants thrive in a mixture of boulders and stones of various sizes that form moraines or screes (see Chapter 5).

In the true alpine region the

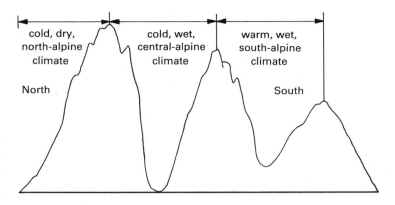

The aspect and climatic conditions in mountain areas will affect the types of alpine plants growing. The successful alpine grower will follow nature's guidelines.

natural climate, depending on the altitude and location, often consists of very short growing seasons and extremes. Air temperatures fluctuate greatly. Sunny south-facing slopes are rapidly warmed by the sun's rays during daytime and cool quickly at night. As a result, soil temperatures are often 2°-4°C warmer at 7,000 ft (2,125 m) than average air temperatures. Shady regions, such as north-facing crevices, can be considerably colder, and offer a home to an entirely different range of plants that are equally well suited to the exposed north-facing garden. At high altitudes rainfall decreases rapidly and during summer many plants only receive light mists. In the autumn snow arrives, air temperatures drop rapidly and plants are sealed in a clean, dry cocoon until the following spring, when the warm sun rapidly thaws retreating snows, flooding the plants and

forcing them into growth. Many of them flower within a few days of emerging from the receding snow line.

The keen alpine grower wanting a continual display of colour should be aware of this spring blooming period and select plants accordingly. A further point is that thick coverings of snow provide an insulation layer, and temperatures at soil level under deep snows are often considerably warmer than shallow falls. The biggest enemy to many garden alpines is, therefore, a wet soil which freezes without a snow covering; so any surplus snow from paths, etc. can provide added protection during cold spells. In addition, the light spectrum in the mountain regions consists of more blue, violet and ultraviolet than is generally found in this country at lower altitudes. This problem is compounded by urban pollution, which significantly reduces

13

light transmission, restricting the growth of high-region alpines.

Alpines have adapted their habit and shape according to the natural environment. Most are of a low prostrate, or mat, habit, which enables them to live in exposed positions where taller, upright subjects could not survive. This mat-like association of shoots also gives added protection from the drying winds and helps, where necessary, to trap and retain snow. Many mat-forming alpines hug the contours of rocks and may only be a few inches in height.

Root systems are generally extensive and penetrate between cracks and crevices in rocks to a depth of several feet, where small feeder roots abound in a mixture of finely ground rock and decaying organic material. This fact is often overlooked by novices attempting to build rock gardens with poor soil structure and impeded drainage – something that rarely occurs on steep mountainsides.

Besides a reduction in overall height and a mat-like habit, many alpines also have modified leaf structures to help reduce the loss of water from the foliage that would be experienced in the drying winds of the mountain-side. In some cases, foliage has become thickened, as in *Sedum* (stonecrop); and certain alpines like *Leontopodium* (edelweiss) have hairy leaf surfaces, whilst plants such as the saxifrages have chalk glands. In other instances, such as *Roscoea*, plants are herbaceous, dying down in late summer and not reappearing until mountain snows thaw. This may be well into June, so that such plants have a very short growing season.

Some alpine plants have, over the years, given rise to many selected forms and cultivars, many of which have never seen the harsh environment of the wild. Others listed in catalogues may be rock or dwarf plants to be found in a state of nature on hill-sides or rocky slopes where the soil is too poor or the weather too harsh to support larger forms of plant life.

Since all true alpines and other dwarf plants originated in the wild, it makes sense for any gardener to copy, as far as poss-ible, what happens in nature, so that failures will be few and far between.

3. PLANNING WITH ALPINES

If selected carefully, alpines can give colour throughout most months of the year, be it in the form of flower, foliage, fruit, or even seed head. There can be no other range of plants so suited to any garden anywhere in Britain, no matter the size, aspect or type of soil and regardless of the grower's skill.

Before making a start, you should interpret your site and decide how the alpines can best be utilised. You must work out what percentage of the ground available you wish to devote to this fascinating form of minia-ture gardening. And you have to remember that although certain forms of rock gardening require

The author's own formal rock garden photographed in late May.

15

A natural rock garden.

little or no maintenance, others can be very time consuming, especially when collecting seed, or hand-pollinating plants.

Initial costs, such as the price of rocks and purchase of plants, are a further consideration. Beginners are often offered gifts of totally unsuitable plants that are usually given away because they are too rampant. Propagation is not difficult, but most alpine gardeners will begin by purchasing plants from nurseries. It is important to remember that these plants are small and slow-growing, so if the price tag seems mighty high and the plant extremely small, think of the time factor and the problems the

nurseryman will have had raising them. Cost also affects the way in which these plants are to be grown. Many of the cheaper, more common and often rampant forms will thrive and quickly cover the ground well on a flat normal garden site. It is a misconception that alpines must be grown on steeply sloping banks, but some of the more expensive species demand special conditions.

Having considered the amount of time and money available to build and maintain the rock garden, we should now look closely at the site to determine what factors will enhance or limit our garden and in what form we

slopes – the trees may even be in a neighbour's garden. Try to avoid east-facing slopes as these often thaw out rapidly in the early morning sun, causing damage to plants that in the wild would normally be covered with snow. Mark on the plan any shady areas, remembering that at the height of summer these will be considerably smaller than in the depths of winter when the sun is low in the sky and the shadows are long. On heavy or poorly drained soils this can lead to troublesome moss and plant losses.

Most small gardens tend to be rather formal, flat areas, and one possibility is to contour the site by removing the topsoil and stacking it to one side, moulding the levels of the subsoil to look natural, and then replacing the topsoil in an even layer over the site. Avoid building rock gardens against the walls of buildings where the soil level may come as high as the damp-proof course, and do not mound soil up against fences. Sunken paths can introduce important changes in level and provide surplus soil to build rock mounds, but avoid creating natural ponds.

Survey the site for perennial weeds, as these often cause major problems later if not dealt with prior to construction. Systemic or translocated weedkillers based on glyphosate are very effective against most deep-rooted perennials and are best applied during warm, dull weather while weeds are growing actively. Further applications of this weedkiller will normally eradicate even the most persistent perennial weeds.

should build. Even the smallest type of rock garden requires some form of planning, and it is advisable to make rough plans of the site, marking in any permanent features that cannot be moved or altered, such as manholes, fences, etc. Mark in all existing large shrubs and trees, bearing in mind that in the wild alpine plants do not get dripped on from overhanging trees, and that few alpines can tolerate such conditions in the contrived alpine garden.

The ideal site for a natural rock garden will be a gently sloping site without shade from trees, but with the impression of shrubs and trees on the lower

Pulsatilla vulgaris rubra, the red Pasque Flower.

There is no real control, however, for mare's tail or field horsetail (*Equisetum arvense*). Avoid propagating this pernicious weed by chopping it into sections with a spade, cultivator, etc. Certain lawn weeds, particularly those that creep by underground stems, can also cause problems later and care should be taken where turf from an old lawn is being buried during construction. Lawns containing couch grass (*Agropyron repens*) which are to be adjacent to rock gardens are perhaps best completely killed off and reseeded with non-invasive fine grasses.

The drainage on a rock garden is also crucial, and during the planning stage it is a good idea to excavate a number of pits, the width of a spade and approximately two spits (lengths of spade blade) deep, and to examine the soil profile. In some instances it may be necessary to install land drains connected to a suitable outlet approved by the local water authority, but be wary of digging drainage sumps, as once filled with rubble these often retain water, especially on heavy soils. An alternative, where problems are experienced, is to build raised beds, or, to create a pond or water garden at the lowest point.

We have discussed planning for the formal and informal types of rock garden, but there are many other ways in which alpines can be used, and site factors might dictate raised beds, paved areas, alpine troughs, or even alpines in a cold greenhouse. Some of these methods will be examined in detail later.

4. THE ROCK GARDEN

Let us return to the plan and build a small rock garden, the principles of which can be extended to a site of any size. Ideally, rough outline planning should be carried out in late August or September, together with weed control. Remember that weedkillers should be kept well away from any plants to be retained or moved. Mark out the rough outline of beds and rock faces with sticks and pieces of string or hosepipes, making minor adjustments to suit the site and your eye. The area should be thoroughly cultivated during early autumn but avoid the addition of bulky organic material as this only produces excess lush growth and often allows the ground to settle later. Carry out

An informal rock garden at the TV Garden at Kings Heath Park.

any drainage and subsoil works during good weather and avoid mixing topsoil and subsoil. A carefully contoured site will, of course, quickly give the impression of a natural rock garden, whereas a flat, formal site will require careful placement of rocks to create a sense of third dimension or height.

The type of rock to be used should, where possible, be local, as this often matches soil colour. However, many people like to use weathered Westmorland limestone, which is grey and tends to show good strata or natural lines. True Westmorland limestone, normally the scrapings from the surface of the moor, is often in short supply, and usually expensive; an alternative would be to use Cheddar limestone. Granite, an igneous rock, is a much harder stone and more difficult to place effectively in the rock garden. It is available in Scotland, certain areas of Wales and parts of Devon and Cornwall. York stone, as so often seen in the form of kerbs and pavements, has flat strata and can easily be split for natural stone paths, but larger pieces of suitable shape are more difficult to find. One of the most popular types of rock available today is the sandstone, or millstone grit, as found in Sussex, the Cotswolds and parts of Derbyshire. This relatively soft rock weathers more naturally than granite and is more amenable to plant life.

Whilst the cost of rock may not seem extortionate at ex-quarry prices, carriage costs for considerable distances can be unbelievably high. Where only a few rocks are required, it is possible to select your own at better garden centres, provided you have suitable transport and a strong back to remove them. The rule when selecting rocks is that a

An arrangement of planks and rollers is used to move large stones. (Steel-capped safety boots should be worn.)

20

Erodium chamaedryoides roseum 'Bishops Form'.

few large, naturally shaped pieces with good strata are far more effective than many small unusable lumps, and this fact may determine how your rocks are delivered. Rocks are best transported to the site on sack trucks, or in the case of very large rocks, rolled on a number of rollers. Once on site they can be manhandled, using crowbars or levers, and packed in place with soil, but remember safety in the long and short term. Avoid lifting in bad positions which could cause strains and always wear safety shoes and gloves, taking extra care on frozen ground. The cold winter months provide an ideal period for the actual rock garden construction.

The easiest way for the novice

A rock outcrop constructed on a sloping site.

to understand the arranging of rock, is to visit one of nature's rock gardens, such as those in the Derbyshire dales, the Yorkshire moors or the vast open spaces of Scotland. Examine carefully how nature has arranged the rocks in terraces, or outcrops, which retain some form of soil behind. Look closer and you will see lines or cracks in the rock, known as strata, which were formed as the rock was deposited throughout the ages.

In a rock garden it is important to follow these strata, where they exist in rocks such as Westmorland limestone, to create a natural effect and possibly prevent damage by severe weather. Granite, formed by a different method, is in some ways easier to lay. In any event, the faces of rocks, together with the joints, should match, which

takes a good eye to judge. Once the rocks are held in place with well rammed garden soil, any planting pockets can be backfilled with special mixtures of compost to suit any specific groups of plants; otherwise a good garden soil with a little extra sharp grit can be firmed in.

Rock gardens created on gentle slopes are more natural in appearance, though few gardeners are fortunate enough to have naturally sloping sites. It is possible to remove the topsoil from the area and remodel the subsoil as described earlier, allowing the ground to settle before carrying out rock building. I suggest this from experience and also give a word of warning. Friends of mine constructing a natural rock garden on a West Midlands hillside finished almost blocking the canal at the bottom with rocks of up to two tons!

Even even on a flat, uninter-sting site, dullness can to a ertain extent be alleviated by he use of sunken paths, conifers nd other architectural plants. This is 'formal' rock gardening, ompared with 'natural' rock ardening on a slope.

Gentle slopes and depressions can also be created to give a more natural look to this rather contrived form of rock garden-ing, and in the smallest of gardens this arrangement could replace the lawn completely and be surrounded by boardings and paths.

Primula pubescens 'Rufus' will thrive on a well-drained site.

In either type of rock garden, any paths should look natural. Paving constructed of natural stone should always be of the same type as the rock used, planting holes may be left as described in Chapter 13, and any steps should be of an appropriate size. There is little room in the natural rock garden for reconstituted precast concrete paving, but in the formal rock garden this can be worked into the design, especially where the garden is surrounded by rectangular panels of fencing, etc. Stone chippings, ideally of *irregular* size, up to ½ in, though extremely difficult to find, can provide a harmonious surrounding to rock beds and should be of the same type as the rock used for construction and, ideally, of irregular sizes.

Existing soil can be improved by the addition of ⅛-½ in grit, concreting sand and, on light soil, peat. On clay soil, peat and other bulky materials, though invaluable for the retention of moisture, may induce moss, a major problem among the mat-forming alpines and something to be avoided. Special pockets can be made of acid or alkaline compost to accommodate those plants with more exacting requirements (see Chapter 19).

Planting normally takes place during April and May and plants are best planted in drifts, using several of one type to form groups which are more effective than many individual plants. When selecting plants, always read the label carefully and study the habit of the plant in question. One of the great skills in planting rock gardens is the selection of plants which will grow harmoniously together and provide colour throughout the twelve months of the year. Avoid putting two plants of creeping habit together as they often become entwined and difficult to keep under control; beware also of rampant mat-forming plants which will quickly invade and kill more choice plants. Space out the plants after ensuring root balls are moist and then plant with a trowel. Remove any weeds and algae from around the neck of the plants which must be planted at the same depth as when growing in the pot. Firm plants in and water in afterwards to settle the soil. Remember that alpines need space to live and grow happily. Some suggestions for different sites in the rock garden are included in Chapter 19, but these are only guidelines as plant fashions change and new plants are bred and introduced. For general maintenance, see Chapter 16.

5. Screes and Moraines

The terms scree and moraine are often confused. A scree is a section of the mountainside that has collapsed and fallen some considerable distance until reaching a suitable resting point. Here, the larger sections of rock will have formed a base, trapping the smaller sections of varying size together with a small percentage of organic matter torn from the mountainside by the rock fall. A number of plants will also have been wrenched from their precarious positions and a very small percentage will survive. As more organic matter is washed down and trapped between the particles of rock, seeds are transported by various means to the scree and in a short period of time a number of sparse plants will colonise this hostile environment.

A moraine, according to most authorities, originates after the passage of a glacier, which has squeezed and compressed rocks into finer fragments, leaving a few of the harder rocks relatively smooth and rounded. Very often water is found at some considerable depth under moraines, which tend to be of gentle sloping habit and more stable than the true scree which, in the wild, will continue to move and alter shape for many years.

It is very simple to adopt the principles of natural screes and moraines, and so introduce a new concept of alpine gardening into even the smallest plot. Ideally, one requires a gently sloping site that is in full sun, so south- and west-facing sites are perfect. If space permits, the scree or moraine can be an extension of the natural rock garden, cascading down to a lower point. In the West Midlands a number of alpine enthusiasts have dedicated their entire plot to this method of gardening, the most effective being where the front lawn is wholly replaced with a scree.

In the contrived situation of the garden the combined moraine and scree make an outstanding feature that is relatively easy to construct. Given the correct aspect and slope, the only other requirement is a suitable soil on a free-draining site. In the wild, water passes through screes and moraines very quickly, even at the height of spring and early summer thaws, something that is very difficult to copy, especially on heavy soils. Ideally, where the drainage is suspect, a network of drains should be installed, particularly at the lower end where waterlogging could occur. Today there are several plastic variations on the old traditional clay tile or land drain, all of which are more effective and easier to install.

Edinburgh's Royal Botanic Garden has a fine example of a scree garden cascading down from the main rock garden and flanked on either side by gently sloping, finely mown turf with occasional outcrops of rocks.

Scree construction at the Royal Horticultural Society Garden, Wisley.

The scree bed is funnel shaped and masked at the top by dwarf shrubs on either side, giving the effect of a slipped mountainside.

Careful thought should be given to planning and a plan of the site should be made as described in Chapter 3 with all the relevant features marked. Avoid the use of level paths and artificial features as these detract from the beautiful range of plants that can be grown on such a site. Consideration should also be given to the rock type and the nature of the plants to be grown.

Acid-loving plants can be grown among certain types of limestone rock that contain no free lime whilst it may be more difficult to grow lime lovers between some of the porous acidic rocks. Some form of chippings will be required, preferably of the same rock type and of varying size from 1/4-3/4 in. These are harder to obtain than materials such as graded granite, as used on roads, which, being of regular size, appear unnatural. Gravel, sometimes recommended, can look atrocious.

the ingredients will depend on the plants selected and local ground conditions.

If suitable, the excavated top soil can be used, otherwise it will be necessary to buy in a sandy loam to mix with peat and grit. Some prefer sedge peat, but sphagnum gives equally good results and even this can be replaced by sieved leaf mould. The term grit has over the years included a whole range of suitable, and unsuitable, materials but basically hard angular rock-like particles of varying sizes are required. Gritty concreting sand, provided it is lime-free, can be used or fine chippings of up to ½ in would be ideal. A ratio of 50% grit, 25% peat and 25% loam is satisfactory for this lower 6 in. The upper 6 in can be 75% chippings, 12.5% loam and 12.5% leaf mould, or 100% chippings. If this depth seems excessive the layer can be reduced to as little as 2 in deep and the lower layer increased to 10 in, without detriment to most scree plants.

A few rocks are required normally at the sides of the scree, but not completely on the edges, best pointed back into the scree with the rounded faces pointing downhill. Where turf meets the scree, it may be advisable to insert a polythene sheet of heavy gauge to prevent stoloniferous or creeping grasses invading the scree, or soil being washed inwards. Access is best provided with a few rather flat rocks well set into the scree, which facilitates easy maintenance.

Most plants for the scree or moraine form tiny mats, or

The site should be weed free, or treated with a suitable weed-killer, as described in Chapter 3. The plan is then roughly marked out, using canes and lines, adjusting the outline shape where necessary to please the eye. The next stage is to remove the top 12 in of soil and rectify the drainage if necessary. The next 6 in can be excavated and replaced with rubble where drainage problems might occur, otherwise the site can be backfilled with two layers of specially prepared compost. The ratio of

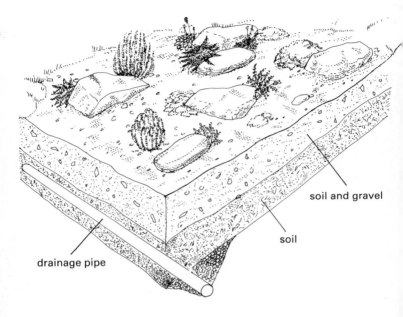

Typical cross-section of scree.

soil and gravel

soil

drainage pipe

hummocks, which enjoy being set on top of the layer of free draining chippings. A list of suitable plants is included in Chapter 19.

When planting, ensure root-balls are moist before placing in a hole in the chippings, which should then be scraped back around the neck of the plant. Once planted, the entire scree should be well watered. Where individual plants are being introduced, the area around the rootball should be thoroughly soaked, as it is the moisture from the chippings which encourages new roots to travel downwards into the prepared layer of loam, peat and grit. It is important, therefore, that all newly planted

alpines in this situation are kep[t] well watered, especially durin[g] the first season.

The maintenance of the scre[e] garden is covered, to a larg[e] extent, in Chapter 16, but ther[e] are one or two minor addition[s]. For instance, where moraine[s] have been constructed, irrigatio[n] can be applied periodically. Th[e] stone chippings tend to mov[e] and from time to time it is necess[-]ary to top up, especially th[e] upper reaches of the beds. Extr[a] care is needed with leaves, whic[h] can quickly become the perfec[t] home for germinating weed see[d] as they rot among the stone[s]. One final warning: small ston[e] chippings lodged under shoe[s] can be carried to surroundin[g]

awn areas, which may cause
antold damage, especially to
cylinder mowers, if not detected
and swept off where necessary
prior to mowing.

Potentilla nitida alba. This is the more unusual white form; a pink variety is freely
available. Both grow to a height of 1 in, forming a hard mat.

6. Dry Walls and Raised Beds

The formation of dry stone walls in any garden offers a third dimension and an extra hard landscape feature, but to the alpine gardener they offer much more. Depending on aspect and soil type, the plant range can be greatly extended, sometimes offering the ideal setting for plants such as lewisias. Any form of wall in the garden that replaces a gradual slope can reduce the dangers and maintenance problems of steep grassy slopes, or eroding soil. The dry wall can be likened to a natural dam clothed with plants. The flat area above offers new possibilities for plants requiring excellent drainage and the flatter area below may be well suited to plants thriving in shade or damp conditions.

The dry wall mound comprises two opposing walls, a certain distance apart, to allow easy maintenance and with suitable end sections to retain soil. If built running east-west, the south side will be a home for sun lovers whilst the north side, with its cool, moist atmosphere, provides the perfect home for plants such as haberleas and ramundas. Being raised above the surrounding ground, most beds of this type are exceedingly free draining. The flat top provides an ideal situation for many alpine gems that are small, finicky and easily lost in the normal rock garden. The fact that the bed is isolated from the surrounding soil also offers the possibility of including plants which require a different pH from that normally found in the garden. For example, the normally acid soil of Edinburgh Royal Botanic Garden houses a fine limestone dry wall which is alkaline in nature, the perfect home for many of the calcifuges or lime-lovers such as the encrusted saxifrages.

Levelling is, in this instance, an important procedure. This can be done by using a builder's spirit-level, a long straight edge, and a number of pegs. Work on a firm base and if necessary lay a shallow footing of concrete to the top of a row of level pegs which should be some 2-3 in below the soil level, to prevent walls settling or falling outwards. To reduce this risk, the wall can be leant slightly backwards, approximately 10°-20° from the vertical, depending on its height and the stone being used.

For dry stone walling, use rectangular or angular rocks which will bond together. Round rocks should be avoided at all costs. Larger key rocks should be selected for the base and then the wall built in layers of suitable thicknesses, gradually reducing the thickness and size of stones, as this looks more natural. However, large key rocks can be used periodically to lock smaller rocks into place and help maintain levels. Soil can be packed between and behind rocks as the wall grows in height. Leave a number of gaps, approximately 3½ in wide, as planting holes, making sure a suitable type of compost is packed in behind the wall at that point. Top off with flattish rocks or stones which will bind lower layers together in a similar way to coping stones on walls.

Dry wall mounds are constructed in a similar way, except in this instance there are several sections of wall, or one long curved wall in the case of the informal dry wall. Try to build up evenly all the way round, again with a slight lean towards the centre of the bed. Depending on the type of rock selected, it may be necessary to cut and trim. This is best done on a heap of soft sand or soil, using a lump hammer and a wide bolster chisel. It is advisable to wear safety glasses or goggles and strong gloves; and don't work

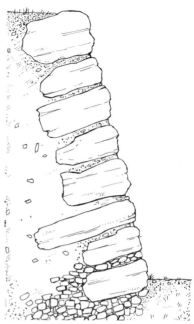

Profile of a dry stone wall.

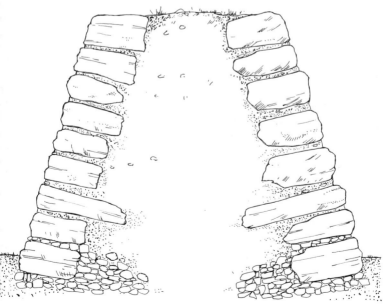

(Below) Profile of a dry stone mound.

31

near windows or greenhouses!

In some instances, attractive raised beds or dry wall mounds can be formed out of broken paving slabs, or other materials such as old timber railway sleepers. However, these are becoming scarce and timber merchants now offer a range of alternatives, such as Junior Sleepers. Reclaimed timbers, including those found in the floors of old maltings, if properly treated against the weather, offer an even cheaper alternative.

Some gardeners may prefer a raised bed constructed of bricks or reconstituted stone blocks. However, there are a few warnings. Do not build a solid brick and mortar walled bed without leaving gaps for drainage. Beds may freeze solid during a bad winter, resulting in the walls being pushed outwards, cracking, and falling over. Where poor underground drainage shows, it is best to install a drain or soakaway before building, and to leave out a number of vertical rows of mortar for drainage, especially at lower levels. On long walls it would be advisable to build either a double skinned wall and/or include a number of piers or pillars, which can finish two to three rows of blocks below soil level. The type of pointing can set off or detract from the bed. When using facing or semi-engineering bricks, a neat, almost flush pointing looks smart, but when using reconstituted stone blocks a number of manufacturers recommend a recessed pointing that is barely visible, so giving the effect of a dry stone wall.

Where dry walls are being built and spaces left for planting, put in pockets of good compost to allow plants to root through without problems. To leave a small hole in the wall for plants

Gentiana acaulis: an ideal plant for a free-draining raised bed.

without thought for the root system is to court failure, especially where walls are in full sun, causing rapid dehydration of the plants. If the planting hole is slightly recessed, the plant can be somewhat shaded, but it may also be out of rain until well established.

Raised beds can be filled with an appropriate planting medium over an adequate drainage base, consisting, say, of gravel chippings or crushed brick. A layer of coarse peat or upturned turves would have been used in the past but today synthetic materials are available in sheet form which allow the water to pass through without the compost blocking the drainage material.

A list of suitable plants is included in Chapter 19 and the planting is very similar to that in the rock garden and with alpine troughs. Where planting is carried out on a near vertical face, a stone, or moulded clay, may be used to keep the plant and the soil behind it in place. A few small rocks can be used on the flatter areas to create a miniature rock garden.

This form of gardening offers considerable scope to the less abled, and careful thought should be given to the design, especially access to, and height of, the bed where older people will be involved in the maintenance. Raised beds offer an ideal easy form of therapy for people with all types of problems, including those with wheelchairs, who will need extra room under the bed. For this purpose precast fibreglass, precast concrete sections, and timber have all been successfully employed. Other people may have difficulty in simply getting down to the plants, and by raising beds to a suitable height they are able to sit or lean on the edge of the bed.

Ramonda growing on a shady, low limestone wall.

7. ALPINE TROUGHS

For many years original stone troughs have been greatly prized amongst alpine enthusiasts for growing choice little gems in literally natural stone. In the early 1930s Clarence Elliott took some pig and horse troughs to Chelsea Flower Show before being banished from the main marquee for such artifices. Stone troughs are nowadays difficult to obtain, expensive and heavy to transport. Furthermore, it is often necessary to drill a number of drainage holes to give at least one square inch of drainage hole to each square foot of trough area. Various alternatives have been tried, some with outstanding success. In the late 1940s and early 1950s many people obtained glazed sinks, often quite deep and with a hideous glaze finish, sometimes using them to grow alpines, and perhaps coating them with a mixture of sharp sand, rubbed sphagnum peat and cement to make them resemble a moss-covered, well-weathered natural stone trough. Experiments have also been made with clay pots of varying designs, fibreglass containers and even secondhand chimney pots. Fine examples can be seen in various gardens where slabs have been placed on breeze blocks, or stone blocks, and edged with small sections of stone to create a table garden effect; indeed large sections of tufa can best be employed in this manner.

The ratio of ingredients is normally taken as 1:1:2, using cement, peat and sand. More sand and less peat leads to a stronger but more concrete-looking trough, whilst increasing the amount of peat gives a moss-covered, soft-textured trough which in severe winters may be prone to frost damage. Glazed sinks should be thoroughly

cleaned and then coated with an adhesive covering such as Unibond. Two or three coats are advised and the last coat may be mixed with sand and cement literally to give a bonding layer.

The sand and cement should be mixed dry and then moistened peat, which has been rubbed through a ⅜ in sieve, added and mixed. When thoroughly combined, water may be added, a little at a time, until the mixture is sufficiently moist to adhere to the vertical walls of a glazed trough. The trough is then given a coating approximately ¾-1 in thick which is firmed into place with gloved hands and trowelled to leave a natural-looking appearance. The trough should then be allowed to dry very slowly; this can be aided by covering with damp hessian sacking, etc.

In the late 1970s I, along with many other people, experimented with the mixture to make troughs by using two cardboard boxes, one placed inside the other, leaving a gap 1½-2 in wide

Two forms of *Phlox douglasi:* Rose Queen (left) Kelly's Eye (right).

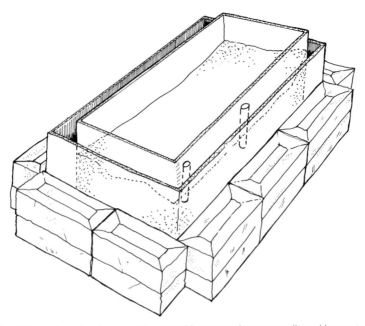

A mixture of sand and cement is poured between the two cardboard boxes to make a trough.

all the way round. Two pieces of broom handle 2 in long are used to provide drainage holes and ensure the bottom is the correct thickness; these will be knocked out at a later date. Alternatively 1 in diameter plastic piping may be used and left in place. The mixture is placed in the bottom of the larger cardboard box and the two broom handle or pipe sections placed in position. The mixture is then consolidated around them as shown in the diagram. The second box is then placed centrally in position and the mixture can be gently eased in between the inner and outer layers of cardboard in layers until full. To prevent the inner one collapsing, bricks and sand may be placed inside as it is necessary to firm down the mixture bet-

ween the inner and outer boxes, using a piece of wood as a rammer. Once completed, the trough is covered again with damp sacking and left to dry slowly.

Two to three days later, the cardboard can be torn off and the sections of broom handle gently tapped out. This is the ideal time to take a wire brush, trowel, etc. and remove outer corners and abrade the trough to give a worn appearance, exposing the peat. The trough will then moss over naturally, and this can be hastened by coating with sour milk, boiled rice water, or ideally, fresh cow manure, especially if left in a grassy, shady place.

One further advance is to use an original trough and take a

moulding, using either fibreglass or vinyl, which has to be melted in a special boiler and poured around the original trough. It is kept in place with a wooden framework around the trough. When set this leaves a rubber-like mould which can be used repeatedly to give an exact replica of the original trough. Colouring agents are available to create sandstone or Cotswold stone-like effects, or alternatively quarried and ground up natural stone may be used to replace the sand; and here, to get the true effect of the stone showing through, white cement should be used.

Planting should be done with great care and any plants selected must be suitably grouped together within the confines of a trough. Invasive plants should be avoided, and sufficient room should always be allowed for plants slowly to grow together. The planting medium is often based on John Innes No. 1 with an additional 30% grit to ensure free drainage. This medium is normally placed over a shallow layer of gravel or broken crocks which in turn may be covered with a woven polythene sheet to prevent the soil fouling the drainage medium. In larger troughs a small rock garden may be created to allow plants the ideal planting environment, but this will depend on the plant selected and the space available.

Juniperus communis 'Compressa' and other very dwarf conifers are ideal for troughs. Remember to select plants according to where the trough is to be placed, taking into account aspect, such as shade, exposure, etc. Indeed, with larger troughs these are best planted *in situ*. Most troughs look best when

Saxifraga oppositipolia 'Ruth Draper' will flower during March and early April.

grouped together and linked with plantings of thymes, saxifrages and sedums, for example. All troughs should be raised off the ground at least 1-2 in to ensure free drainage. Among the most commonly used plants are *Dianthus alpinus* in its various forms and colours, *Globularia bellidifolia*, only 2 in high, with small thistle-like heads of blue during the summer, and the semi-evergreen *Cotoneaster congesta nana*, ideal for creeping over the edge of the trough.

One of the smallest hebes, *Hebe buchananii* 'Minor', is ideal and occasionally offers its small white flowers, and *Veronica teucrium* 'Blue Tit' forms a little trailing mound up to 2 in high and will hang over the front edge of the trough. Of the smaller slower growing saxifrages, per-

haps the best known is *S. cochlearis minor*, forming a small silver dome, whilst *S. oppositifolia* 'Ruth Draper' is one of the best of the trailing forms, providing welcome colour during March and early April. *Phlox douglasii* provides many named forms of bun-like plants that flower in June, such as *P.* 'Kelly's Eye' and there are several even smaller forms.

Plants must not be allowed to go short of water during dry periods. Generally, no feeding is required, and provided suitable plants have been selected at the outset, little or no pruning should be necessary. This, therefore, must make the ideal form of gardening, particularly for those who have little time to spare but want the enjoyment and pleasure of growing rarities.

8. THE ALPINE MEADOW OR LAWN

The spectacle of colourful alpines growing abundantly in short grass can be reproduced in a small garden either by creating a spring meadow underplanted with a range of bulbs or by creating a lawn, with a variety of plants, as part of the rock garden.

The spring meadow, as demonstrated at Wisley, is normally an area of longer grass rather than a high-grade lawn, and might be planted with dwarf daffodils (*Narcissus bulbocodium*) and crocus, although other bulbs can also be used. The grass, however, must be maintained throughout the season. Bulbs will flower and spread naturally provided a 6-8 week period is allowed after flowering before the surrounding grass is cut; this, in most cases, is from mid June or early July through to October or early November. The first cut will usually have to be carried out with a rotary mower, and thereafter with either a rotary or cylinder mower, depending upon the type of finish required. Avoid deep spiking and treat large infestations of weeds mid August with a proprietary hormone weedkiller after applying a fertiliser to ensure grass and weeds are growing well. Do not compost the first two or three mowings.

Selecting and planting bulbs can be carried out in late summer. Site conditions will to some extent dictate the choice.

Some require a hot, dry period to mature, some, like the snowdrop, are happiest on a heavy soil, others may prefer sun, or even a wet site. Broad drifts of similar coloured bulbs should be encouraged; small blocks of differing colours or mixed colours tend to be less effective. Always buy good quality bulbs from a reliable source and remember, as a general guide, that most bulbs should be planted 2-2½ times their depth below the surface.

To obtain a natural look, place the bulbs in a bucket or trug and throw them out over the required area, literally planting them where they fall. A range of bulb planters can be used which will remove a core of soil, enabling larger bulbs to be placed in the bottom of the hole and then re-

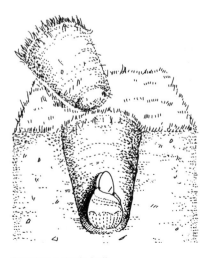

Planting a single bulb.

39

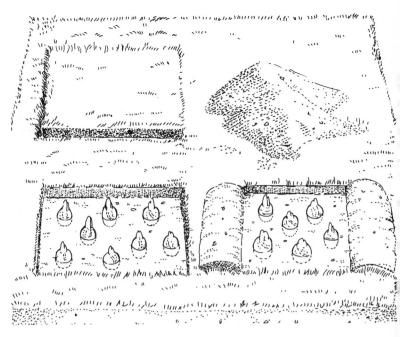

Two methods of planting small pockets of bulbs.

leasing the core back into the hole. For small pockets of crocus, etc., an edging iron may be employed to cut a letter 'H' into the turf and then a spade or turf float used to peel the turf back from either side of the centre cut. The bulbs are then placed in position and the turf relaid. Bulbs may also be planted with a trowel or crowbar and, if necessary, a little grit or sand added to the planting hole to ensure that planting is at the correct depth and that the bulb has free drainage. Recently a number of bulb fertilisers have come on the market and these may be used at the time of planting.

Planting under trees may be more difficult, and sometimes it is advisable to use young plants grown in pots, as in the case of cyclamen under beech trees.

Care should be taken when planting bulbs among the roots of rhododendrons, magnolias, etc. Do this at an early stage, while the shrubs are small, to minimise root damage. Avoid planting under conifers and privet hedges. Make sure, too, that turf, cores, etc. are firmly replaced, leaving no air pockets or spaces for mice to devour next year's flower display.

Little or no maintenance of such areas is required. Where bulbs become overcrowded, flowering will be reduced, so lift them in the autumn, having previously marked the area during the flowering period. Bulbs should be divided, spaced according to variety, and surplus bulbs lined out for future use or given away. Snowdrops are one of the few bulbs that should be lifted complete with foliage, immediately after flowering, divided and replanted as soon as possible. All bulbs will benefit from a low nitrogen, high phosphate/potash feed after flowering to promote growth for the following season. Remember not to cut the green foliage off or to tie the foliage in a knot, as this prevents bulb development.

For an alpine lawn, the basic principle is to create a mat-like area among rock outcrops, etc. Given a suitable suite free of perennial weeds and very free-draining, plus a few carefully placed, flattish stepping stones, a lawn-like appearance can be created with a wide variety of plants.

Perhaps the most useful of plants to clothe a heavily used area is the native creeping thyme (*Thymus serpyllum*), together with its numerous varieties, some of which are only 2 in high when in flower. Others are a little taller, and a few have hairy grey foliage, making the plants most attractive when not in flower. There are a number of good forms of the

Fritillaria are scattered throughout this beautiful alpine meadow.

A traditional alpine lawn at the Royal Botanic Gardens, Edinburgh.

lemon thyme (*Thymus* × *citriodorus*) with yellow variegated foliage which, as with most other thymes, when walked upon provides a pleasant scent.

Among many other mat-forming plants which may also be used to form a lawn, are the acaenas, often too invasive for the small rock garden. *A. microphylla*, with its bronzy leaves and red burr-like flowers, grows only to 2 in and is similar to *A. buchanani*, which is green and slightly more rampant. The antennarias, with woolly grey foliage and pink flowers in June, quickly form large mats, as do the achilleas, but remember to choose only dwarf forms such as *Achillea lewisii*. Other plants worth considering include *Silene acaulis*, only 1 in high, with pink flowers in June, *Potentilla nitida*, with rose pink flowers and attractive seed heads, and several members of the veronica family, to name but a few.

Members of the thyme family are ideal to use for lawns since they are easily propagated and one stock plant will often provide many Irish cuttings (partly rooted). These can be planted at 4-6-in centres, according to vigour, and will quickly form large mats. Other plants, such as the antennarias, can be lifted and divided to obtain sufficient plants to cover the area quickly. Little maintenance is required once plants have formed a lawn-like appearance. Germinating weed seedlings should be removed at the earliest opportunity and seedheads occasionally trimmed with shears. Under-planting with bulbs can provide colour throughout most of the season, and there is an ever increasing range of dwarf tulips and crocus. Ants may cause considerable damage to the roots of thymes while feeding on aphids. Dusting with a Permethrin-based powder is normally effective.

9. WATER IN THE ROCK GARDEN

In mountainous regions there is always a rush of water downhill particularly after thaws, rains, etc. But there are also quiet places where water collects in small pools or boggy marshes, and it is important to try to copy some of the basic rules encountered in the wild when adding water to the contrived rock garden. Water always finds the lowest point and should be in scale with the size of the garden. It is sometimes necessary to carry out excavations, using surplus soil to create rock gardens around the pool feature. There is an attraction in moving water but to do this it is necessary to install a pump to recycle it, and it may be difficult to create a natural-looking series of pools without losing water.

Today there are a number of alternative materials that can be used for pools in addition to clay or concrete, both of which have drawbacks. Preformed fibreglass pools were for some years the favourite alternative for small gardens, but several synthetic materials which do not become brittle in sunlight or puncture easily are now available, and perhaps the most outstanding of these is butyl. This is available in several thicknesses and can generally be supplied, with a 15-year guarantee, welded together in rolls to form sheets of the required size. Cheaper alternatives are reinforced PVCs which have a life expectancy of 5-10 years and are unaffected by sunlight and fungi. It is advisable to instal liners of any kind on polyester matting in order to cushion the effect of sharp stones or rough edges in the case of raised pools. Liners should always be at least 2 ft larger than the overall area, plus twice the depth of the pool, so as to allow them to be brought up behind the initial layer of rocks and well above the proposed water level.

The pool should be marked out with a hosepipe, loosely laid in the shape planned, and minor adjustments made to suit the eye and the terrain and to ensure that the pool sits at the lowest point. Excavated soil may be used to create rock mounds but subsoil should be kept purely for building and topsoil utilised for clothing mounds evenly to permit planting. It is handy to use a builder's long spirit level in conjunction with a straight edge and a number of long pegs; these can be knocked in to the proposed water level and the spirit level used to guarantee that all pegs are at exactly the same level. The pool should have gently sloping sides and the edges masked with rocks or paving, which should overhang the rim. Alternatively, an alpine bog garden can be formed by bringing the liner up to the surface and then gently forming a depression before bringing it again to the surface some feet away.

A simple waterfall construction with surrounding rockery.

The same technique can be employed to create a series of rock pools, remembering to bring the liner up well behind the rocks forming the side of the pool. A spirit level should be used to set in position the rocks over which the water will cascade. During construction a hosepipe should be buried to take water from a submerged pump in the lower pool to the pool at the top of the stream.

Concrete pools require treatment before planting, but those constructed of liners can be planted immediately with various groups of plants. One major problem is to keep the water clear, and this can be achieved by the correct balance of plants to the surface area of the pool. As a general guide, this is only practical with pools of over 50 square feet where 60% of this surface area can be covered by plants.

Water or aquatic plants can be classified into the following groups: submerged, floating, oxygenating, marginal and surrounding.

In the deeper areas submerged plants can be grown in baskets, and plants such as water-lillies should be selected according to the water depth. For large pools 2-4 ft in depth, *Nymphaea* 'Escarboucle' with its large red flowers will quickly cover the area, while pools 1-3 ft deep, are ideal for *N.* 'James Brydon', a best seller with rich rose-pink flowers, or *N.* 'Marliacea', with soft yellow flowers. In shallow pools 9-18 in deep one can plant *N. froebeli* with crimson red flowers, or *N. lilacea* with light mauve-pink flowers. Even the smallest of pools can accommodate *N. pygmaea* and its cultivars, provided 6-9 in of water depth is available.

Other deep-water plants include *Aponogeton distachyos* (water hawthorn) with white scented flowers, and *Sagittaria sagittifolia* (arrowhead) with white flowers in July. In water 2-6 in deep one can plant the small reed mace, *Typha minima*, and *Acorus calamus-variegatus*, with dwarf iris-like foliage 6-8 in high. *Caltha palustris* (marsh marigold) and *Mysotis palustris* (water orget-me-not) are happiest in very shallow water and mud. It is important that oxygenating plants such as *Miriophyllum proserpinaoides* (parrot's feather), should be planted in trays at a rate of one per 3 sq ft of water.

Although few marginals are true alpines, many are suited to the conditions around the pool. Astilbes range from 3 in upwards, as do the newer dwarf hostas. *Polygonum affine* can hide the edge of rock streams, while the primula family offers many gems such as *P. rosea* and *P. denticulata*. A number of the dwarf willows (*Salix*) are quite happy to creep over the edges as are the miniature cotoneasters, but one of my favourites is *Lysimachia nummularia* 'Aurea', the golden-leaved creeping jenny.

There are many taller plants that are at home around the edge of ponds, such as the candelabra primulas, *Gunnera manicata* with its giant rhubarb-like leaves, or one of the many ornamental grasses. These are outside the scope of this book but it is always worthwhile remembering that no garden feature is complete without a backcloth, preferably of larger plants.

The water garden diary begins in early April, when pool heaters can be disconnected and put away, and, if necessary, pools half-emptied and refilled with fresh water. Fish can be fed, depending on the water temperature. May sees the planting season in full swing. Never use nitrogen-rich soil for planting baskets as this turns the water

A small artificially-created pond with rock falls.

green. When this happens, do not change the water but let nature take her course; provided the balance of plants is right, ponds will normally clear of their own accord.

June sees the first water-lillies in flower. Stocking can continue with plants and fish, which should be left floating in the supplier's polythene bag to allow equalisation of water temperatures between bag and pond, and preventing shock or even death of fish. Normally after twenty minutes, bags can be opened and the fish allowd to swim out. During July the water should be circulated to prevent oxygen deficiency and the pool regularl topped up with water. Augus should be a month for relaxing and enjoying the pond, bu beware of thunderstorms an always run the circulating pum to oxygenate ponds.

September can see late pon planting, particularly in warme areas. The next few weeks ar also critical to fish. They shoul not be allowed to go short of foo and where ponds are likely to b affected by falling leaves it i advisable to cover with a fine mesh net. The pond heate should also be installed during the autumn in anticipation o colder weather.

10. THE WILD GARDEN

The term 'wild garden' may conjure up ideas of a perfect rock garden in the wild – difficult to achieve in Britain where there are few true alpine regions. But the Royal Botanic Gardens, such as Edinburgh, have very successfully created the 'managed' wild garden. This is an area which requires semi-conventional maintenance and the observance of a few basic rules of conservation. In the perfect wild garden a climax vegetation would spring up after a number of years, i.e. the most dominant and powerful species would take over. In theory, little or no management would take place, except in the form of grazing animals, etc. But in the average garden, some control obviously has to be exercised.

A trip into Lincolnshire will show cowslips growing abundantly on roadside embankments, while in Scotland *Silene acaulis* can be seen along with stonecrop, growing happily together in competition with the surrounding vegetation. Primulas, for instance, given suitable soil conditions, will hold their own amongst other favourable vegetation. But there are a number of weeds, including the common dock, that would quickly dominate damp areas such as those favoured by *Primula pulverulenta*.

The solution is to create, by traditional gardening methods, an area that is weed-free and well cultivated, to plant suitable species in bold groups, and to wait for the problems to occur. When one planting appears to be getting out of control or is being invaded by weeds, it is time to take action and redress the balance.

The theme of the wild garden could encompass almost any angle of rock gardening, but be warned; in the ideal conditions of a peat garden, for instance, certain desirable plants such as *Uvularia grandiflora* can become weeds by invading other plants vegetatively or by seeds.

Many plants found in alpine meadows, such as *Primula scotica*, grow happily in association with grass and other herbs. Orchids, too, thrive with grasses and other roadside vegetation, but are difficult to keep alive in the garden – an excuse perhaps for not weeding, and certainly an argument for conservation.

Opposite Meconopsis: an ideal plant for the 'managed' wild garden.

11. THE WOODLAND GARDEN

The alpine woodland affords unlimited scope to the gardener who possesses a number of trees. It offers exciting and varying conditions such as full sun, dappled or light shade, and heavy shade, providing cool summer conditions and protection from harsh winter winds. In the wild the soil type is often acid, due to the falling leaves of a wide range of trees, including members of the silver birch and pine families, and many other conifers. And the woodland garden may also attract wildlife beneficial to the gardener, notably birds which eat harmful pests.

The open sunlight position can sometimes be blended wit dense shade by means of the pe: garden methods as described i Chapter 12, or alternatively b using more of the woodland-typ plants that are happier in th shade rather than full su: Indeed, many shade lovers, espe cially variegated forms, wi decline if planted in a sunn position. Conversely, variegate plants that normally need fu sun will become very drawn an weak, and prone to disease planted in heavy shade.

In an alpine woodland, dapple shade is often provided by smal leaved trees such as birch. In th garden it is important to avoi large-leaved trees, such as syca

The effect of summer and winter sun on the area of shade beneath a deciduous tree. In winter, although the shaded area is larger, more sunlight will get throug to the plants beneath as the tree will have lost its leaves.

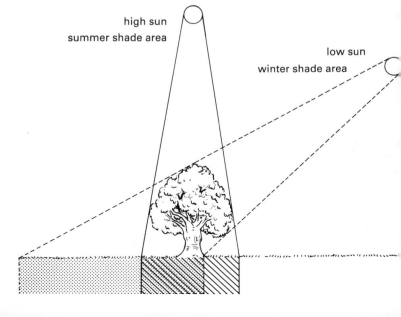

high sun
summer shade area

low sun
winter shade area

The Woodland Garden.

ore which, in the autumn, shed
 thick layer of leaves that covers
nd kills smaller plants under-
eath. During summer decid-
ous woodlands can offer consid-
rable shade, but in winter
nderplantings receive substan-
ally more sunlight. In the case
f spreading low-branched trees,
ne weight of foliage, especially
fter rain, may bring branches
own on to underplantings.

The spacing of trees also needs
 be taken into account. In
lpine woodland, tree density is
ften low, allowing sunlight to
enetrate at certain times of the
ay. The closer the trees, the less
ght is able to reach the under-
lanting.

Ideally, underplanting of dwarf
hrubs, herbs and bulbs should
e carried out in conjunction
ith tree planting, as it is ex-

tremely difficult to establish new
plants under the canopy of older
trees with existing root systems.
Most woodland plants are surface rooting and feed on the
decaying matter from the autumn
leaf falls. Bearing this in mind, it
is advisable to allow the natural
composting of leaves where they
fall, provided this does not cause
damage to any of the underplantings. This natural compost can
be supplemented with additional
top dressings of leaf mould or
home-made compost. The forming of raised beds should be
avoided, as these tend to dry out.

An alpine woodland effect can
be created under a shrub border
or even a small single tree, gradu-
ating from plants requiring full
sun to those needing shade.
Plants may be established in
weed-free grass, or a traditionally

49

cultivated border, using normal gardening techniques.

The range of plants is most extensive, including a number of North American and Canadian woodland plants such as *Cornus canadensis*, and the trilliums. Not all may be strictly called alpines, but some provide attractive flowers, foliage and fruit that would perhaps be difficult to place elsewhere in the garden. The following are suitable for various types of shade.

Ajuga reptans (bugle). Excellent ground cover with variegated foliage for moist soils.

Anemone. Various forms are suitable, especially *A. nemorosa* (wood anemone), *A. blanda* and *A. apennina*, all flowering in early spring.

Arisaema triphyllum (jack in the pulpit). Unusual N. American plant with brown spotted green and white spathe, flowering in summer.

Arisarum proboscideum (mouse plant). Forms carpets of green foliage with brown mousetail-like flowers in early summer.

Arum italicum. Ideal for a shady spot in grass; marbled leaves and spikes of red berries in autumn.

Cortusa matthioli. Requires similar conditions to *Primula cortusoides* section and flowers in early summer; various shades from white to deep pink.

Cyclamen hederifolium. Rose-pink flowers in Sept., followed by marbled foliage.

Disporum smithii. Creamy-green flowers in spring and large orange berries in late summer; an unusual plant for a shady, cool spot.

Erythronium (trout lily). Several forms are well suited to the woodland garden and produce yellow or white flowers in spring. *E. dens-canis* (dog's tooth violet), with deep rose pink flowers in March, also forms good ground cover.

Galanthus (snowdrop). Can provide flower from Oct. to April; happy on most soils provided peat and humus are available.

Glaucidium palmatum. A Japanese woodlander with large leaves and hellebore-like mauve or white flowers in late spring.

Hepatica nobilis. Ideal for peaty soil with blue or occasionally pink flowers, overlobed leaves in March or April.

Lilium. Many forms of the lily are happy in a humus-rich, well-drained soil where roots and bulbs can remain undisturbed, whilst flowers receive dappled sunlight.

Meconopsis (poppy). Many forms suited to the larger woodland garden with blue, red, yellow or occasionally white flowers, some monocarpic, i.e. dying after flowering. The best perennial poppy, with large sky-blue flowers, is *M.* × *sheldonii*.

Primula, especially *P. japonica*, *P. pulverulenta*, and *P. sieboldii* which is deciduous.

Saxifraga fortunei 'Wada's Form'. Deep purple foliage and white flowers in early autumn.

12. THE PEAT GARDEN

Peat gardening offers a new and exciting method of growing plants that are not always strictly alpines in today's small gardens. In contrast to the traditional rock garden, its purpose is to create a new environment for a wide range of small beautiful plants which until recently had been considered relatively difficult to grow. Fine examples of established peat gardens are to be found in the Logan Botanic Gardens, near Stranraer, in Edinburgh Royal Botanic Garden (where peat walls accommodate a range of plants from the Himalayan regions, Japan, South Africa, America and Europe), at Wisley, in Kew Gardens, in Liverpool Botanic Gardens at Ness, and at Harlow Carr, which is the home of the Northern Horticultural Society in Harrogate.

Unlike a rock garden, peat gardens are built from sections of peat blocks, usually 6-8 in thick, 12-18 in long and 6-8 in high, which are built into retaining walls in a bonded pattern similar to a brick wall. Peat blocks are very amenable to plant life and the roots of many peat-loving plants will run through the blocks, knitting them together and transforming them into an integral part of a growing

The Gentiana sino-ornata flowers from late August to October.

garden, masked by plants and mosses.

Peat gardening is ideally suited to the typical suburban garden surrounded by 6 ft fence panels and shaded for at least part of the day. A peat garden can be sited in a very small space and is perfect for north sites of buildings; and although never successful directly under the canopy of trees, it may be positioned on the shady side of trees and shrubs. Another attraction is the fact that peat blocks are relatively light-weight and easily handled; and if the charm wears off after a number of years, the blocks can either be burnt on the barbecue or broken up and incorporated into the soil. It is not so easy to dispose of several tons of rock.

One of the major enemies of the peat garden is the stoloniferous type weed (a creeping weed or plant growing in the wrong place) since once established it will be impossible to use selective weedkillers, or to dig out. Certain less desirable plants, if sited on or near the peat wall, will become as invasive as couch grass. Many of the plants used in the peat garden resent any disturbance at all and some are very surface rooting. So it is best to remove all weed seedlings as early as possible by hand; larger perennial weeds may be eased out with a hand fork, never with a hoe or border fork. Some weeds, such as *Cardamine hirsuta* (bitter cress), produce vast quantities of seed only a few weeks after germinating themselves and should be speedily removed. Others are plants that have produced vast quantities of viable seed which have germinated beyond control following a mild winter. Some plants, such as *Uvularia sessilifolia*, send out stolons through the peat bed and come up through the most choice plants or destroy the peat blocks. The answer here is to be very selective when choosing plants and not to jump at gifts from friends.

The peat garden offers a new microclimate that will accommodate a very wide range of plants. Wet peat moistens and cools the atmosphere in the

vicinity and many woodland plants revel in this freshness. The soil should be slightly acid, e.g. pH 5.5-6.5 or, at the very least, neutral (pH 7). Few peat gardens are established on alkaline or limy soils, but even using a technique of isolating the peat bed by raising it up has its shortcomings. The local water supply (which is usually alkaline) often has to be used to irrigate the peat bed and this can cause the death of many plants.

In order to provide a cool summer environment, the soil must be moisture retentive yet free-draining; and if necessary, drains should be installed as no peat-loving plants will tolerate waterlogged conditions. A gentle sloping site is ideal, but ensure that the lower part is not a frost pocket, since this could have devastating effects on choice, otherwise hardy, plants that are just coming into growth. A little shade is desirable, but heavy shade from overhead canopies should be avoided, and drips from trees can cause disaster. On the other hand, the shelter pro-

A large-scale peat garden at the Royal Botanical Gardens, Edinburgh.

vided by a reduced wind speed through surrounding shrubs, etc. is beneficial, especially on the east coast where cold drying winds can damage many plants.

Droughts may cause problems in spring and at other times in the growing season, so lime-free water should be available to keep the peat moist and the atmosphere cool. Care should be taken to ensure that the blocks do not become tinder dry and fuel-like, as this may kill the mosses and disintegrate the peat blocks. Heavy pounding with large droplets of water from irrigation hoses should be avoided and sprinklers should be set to give a fine mist.

Freshly cut peat blocks can be difficult to obtain, nor is it legal to cut your own locally without the necessary licences. The alternative is to obtain barbecue blocks which should then be placed in an empty dustbin, a hose pipe inserted and the lid firmly tied on. The bin should be filled and then regularly topped up until the blocks will absorb no more water.

The completed peat garden should, in theory, resemble a fissured, gauged moorland with terraces and walls. It is essential to start with a weed-free site and any perennial weeds treated with a translocated weedkiller. The site should then be shaped and contoured as described in Chapter 3. Peat blocks can be installed to simulate an informal curving brick wall and in order to maintain stability blocks should lean backwards into the higher soil levels. Walls should be allowed to flow, rising and falling

with the contours of the land, and, where appropriate, can disappear into the rise of the slope. If necessary, blocks can be cut to shape with an old panel saw, and once in place should be gently firmed from behind so as to leave no air spaces.

Sphagnum peat should be worked into the soil to produce a peaty acid soil and, where necessary, flowers of sulphur can be added to the soil in an attempt to lower the pH. The soil should be lightly firmed and stepping stones laid in the terraces to facilitate weeding and other cultural operations. Once construction is completed, the whole area can be given a thorough watering and allowed to drain and settle.

The environment provided by a peat garden is suited to a very wide range of plants and it is important to consider the forms needed for a successful balance of plant material before selecting individual items. Shrubby material will provide shelter from winds, whilst evergreens provide shelter and form especially during winter. Herbaceous plants and bulbs provide a welcome break from shrubby material, whereas creeping and mat-forming plants help to suppress weed seedlings. Avoid overplanting with shrubby material which may in time grow together to form an impenetrable barrier.

The peat garden offers a perfect home to dwarf lilies, with their feet in the shade and the flowers in the sun, among dwarf rhododendrons, while the front of the border may be occupied by small, often herbaceous plants, together with dwarf bulbs.

The soil should be gently firmed prior to planting but not over-consolidated. Shrubs can be established in the autumn but much of the herbaceous material is best left until spring. Many plants are surface rooting and special attention should be paid to correct planting depth, which should then be followed by a generous watering to settle the plants in.

The maintenance of the peat wall is relatively simple; the only tools required are a hand fork and a pair of secateurs together with a bucket for weeds, etc. Generally it is only a matter of weeding, clearing up twigs and debris, pruning out deadwood and flower heads, and seed collecting, if required, bearing in mind that seed production is at the expense of plant growth.

In nature the peat garden is regularly topped up with decaying matter provided by falling leaves, erosion, etc. Compensate for this by applying a thin layer of peat, or similar material, preferably in spring, together with the slightest dusting of a general fertiliser on hungry soils, as most peat-loving plants require little feeding.

Even without feeding, some creeping plants can become rampant under the ideal conditions of a peat garden. It may become necessary to control their size by pruning and, where choice plants are being crowded out, to remove second-rate competitors which are swamping them.

The peat garden can be ablaze in the autumn with leaf colour, gentians, etc., but the effect of soggy leaves falling on many of the smaller plants may be disastrous. Fine netting stretched over the peat wall can be used to trap leaves which, periodically shaken off on to paths or turf, are far easier to collect.

Some plants such as the rarer Asiatic primulas may require overhead protection against moisture forming in the resting buds, and this can be provided by sheets of glass or plastic, edged with plastic insulation tape for safety, and resting on wires to keep them in place.

In general terms, though there are many variable factors, such as soil type, rainfall, amount of shade and even the possible supply of plants, the peat garden or wall offers the ideal home to many members of the Ericaceae family such as *Rhododendron, Cassiope, Andromeda, Chamaedaphne,* and *Enkianthus.* The family Liliaceae covers many beautiful bulbs which fit in well with shrubby plants as most are deep rooting and resent disturbance. The Primulaceae family includes not only a wide range of primulas but also a number of beautiful primula-like plants such as *Omphalogramma, Dodecatheon* and *Cyclamen.*

The table on page 56 has been compiled in order to help you in the choosing of suitable plants for growing in a peat garden. These plants come from the Ericaceae, the Liliaceae and the Primulaceae families. A second table below lists the members of other families which might well be possible candidates for the peat garden.

Ericaceae	Liliaceae	Primulaceae
Andromeda	*Bulbinella*	*Cortusa*
Arctostaphylos	*Clintonia*	*Cyclamen*
Bruckenthalia	*Disporum*	*Dodecatheon*
Bryanthus	*Erythronium*	*Omphalogramma*
Calluna	*Fritillaria*	*Primula*
Cassiope	*Helonias*	
Chamaedaphne	*Lilium*	
Daboecia	*Liriope*	
Enkianthus	*Nomocharis*	
Epigaea	*Notholirion*	
Erica	*Paris*	
Gaultheria	*Polygonatum*	
Kalmia	*Smilacina*	
Ledum	*Tricyrtis*	
Leiophyllum	*Trillium*	
Menziesia		
Pernettya		
Phyllodoce		
Phyllothamnus		
Rhododendron		
Vaccinium		

Members of other families

Adonis	*Epimedium*	*Paeonia*
Arisaema	*Fothergilla*	*Platycodon*
Arisarum	*Galanthus*	*Polygala*
Arum	*Gentiana*	*Polygonum*
Asarum	*Glaucidium*	*Pyrola*
Astilbe	*Hacquetia*	*Ranunculus*
Boykinia	× *Heucherella*	*Romanzoffia*
Calanthe	*Hylomecon*	*Salix*
Calceolaria	*Incarvillea*	*Sanguinaria*
Codonopsis	*Linnaea*	*Saxifraga*
Cornus	*Meconopsis*	*Shortia*
Corydalis	*Mertensia*	*Synthyris*
Cyananthus	*Orchis*	*Tanakaea*
Cyathodes	*Ourisia*	*Thalictrum*
Cypripedium	*Pachysandra*	

13. Paved Alpine Areas

Lawns normally require considerable maintenance, what with cutting, feeding, weedkilling, spiking and scarifying. On the other hand, lawn areas can be paved over to provide interesting, relatively maintenance-free features which can be greatly enhanced by planting with suitable mat-forming alpines. Initially, the cost of buying and laying paving may seem rather frightening, but areas around the house can be turned into alpine patios and walled areas can be turned into alpine courtyards. The use of rectangular slabs can provide a formal atmosphere, whilst crazy or natural paving can provide the perfect setting for troughs, raised beds, etc. Furthermore, all paved areas provide a cool root run under slabs.

The choice of paving types and materials which can be used is most extensive and it is worth considering the use of old street paving, tiles, hard or semi-engineering bricks, even old factory floor stones. There is also a broad range of reconstituted stone or concrete based precast paving, including many natural looking finishes.

When planning an alpine paved area, it is essential to remember that alpines dislike waterlogged conditions. Care should be taken to ensure that the site is free draining and that water will not collect in the specially prepared planting pockets. In some instances this may mean installing a network of drains below the paved area, connected either to a soakaway or the local storm water system, as described earlier.

If you are starting from scratch, draw a plan of the area, with the proposals on a sheet of tracing paper which can be laid over the plan. As in the case of the alpine beds, dig out a profile pit, examine the soil type and consider the use and weights the paving will have to take. Depending upon these factors, you will need a base of hardcore or stone of appropriate thickness which is then blinded, or covered, with a layer of sand. The slabs should be laid either directly on a further layer of sand, dusted with a liberal application of cement, then raked in lightly and levelled. Slabs can be laid on this bed which will set like concrete after the first rains. Alternatively, a mixture of concreting sand and cement (1:5) can be made up and a trowelfull placed under each corner and the centre of each slab, which in turn is tapped down to the correct levels.

Paths near houses should have a slight fall away from the building and should always be below the level of the damp course. Other areas may be laid without a cross fall but since water can collect and freeze during winter months, leading to cracking, especially on natural stone areas, the pointing between sections of stone should be flush, or slightly higher than the paving. (Some authorities disagree with this practice and argue that pointing between slabs should finish below the surface of the slab in a recessed manner, similar to a dry stone wall.) Certain patterns of reconstituted paving require pointing between their irregular shapes, while the more traditional slabs can be butted together. The

Cobble inserts and reproduction paving can bring a modern touch.

A combination of irregular natural stone and pre-cast concrete sections have been used to form this paved area.

careful combination of slabs of differing sizes can lead to a most pleasing effect, but it is best to use the manufacturer's guides and plans to ensure no unwanted gaps are left.

Paved areas look more interesting with steps to give a change of level, and dry stone walls, as described earlier, can retain soil and paving where necessary. When building steps, remember to make the flat area large enough for feet and the rise between steps convenient for people of all ages. The actual step should always overhang the rise by an inch or so. Steps should always be cemented in firmly to avoid accidents.

Certain types of new pavers can be covered with well-rotted, watered-down cow manure to speed the ageing process, encourage lichen and create a more pleasing effect.

The planting pits must connect with the underlying soil below the paving so that the plant roots can reach the soil and allow the surface water to drain away. To avoid torrents of water pouring down planting holes, the surrounding paving may be fractionally higher, or have a cross-fall away from the planting pit. Where butt joints are used, water will often drain away between slabs.

The actual mixture in the planting pits will depend upon the aspect and the plants selected. As a rule these pits require better drainage than similar sites in alpine beds. On sandy sites little preparation, other than filling the planting pocket, is needed; but on clay soils considerable care is required to ensure that the planting hole does not become a wet, spongy pocket.

Plants selected for this area should be capable of withstanding occasional passage of feet in the case of mat-forming plants such as thymes. Other suitable plants include the acaenas from New Zealand with their attractive burr-like flowers, *Antennaria dioica* rosea at 2-3 in high and *Cotula squalida* at 1 in. *Dryas octopetala minor* forms a woody mat at only 1 in while *Erinus alpinus* with its pink and mauve flowers will seed itself freely in the paving cracks. *Mentha requienii*, creeping among the smallest cracks, gives off a most attractive scent when crushed and occasionally offers mauve or white flowers. Some more upright shrubs, such as *Hydrangea* 'Pia', will provide flower in late summer and mat-forming shrubs such as *Cytisus* can be used where space permits. In all cases try to site plants out of direct lines of walking, planting around troughs, seats and at the side of steps.

Planting may require a little ingenuity to place the root ball below the paving without the crown of plants being so low as to rot off, especially when debris collects in planting pockets. Bulbs may be used in larger pockets; and all pockets may be topped off with chippings, if required. Once established, little maintenance is required, as most plants are pruned by passing feet. Shrubs and more vigorous plants can, if necessary, be pruned. Due to the surface water from the paved area, little watering is needed and because of the isolated nature of plants, few pests and diseases appear.

14. Alpines in the Greenhouse

For the keen alpine enthusiast and the novice alike, the greenhouse opens up a whole new range of possibilities. Anyone with a heated or partially heated greenhouse knows that during winter, regardless of the heating method, bills quickly soar. With alpines, however, there is no need for heating, the only requirement being that the air is kept dry during the winter months, which can be achieved by the use of electric fan heaters or tubular electrical heaters. Because condensation of the glass can be detrimental to the health of choice alpines, full ventilation should be used whenever the opportunity arises; but in the event of damp or wet weather, some form of drying of the air is advisable.

The actual type of greenhouse used for the growing of alpines is very much up to the individual grower. In the past the purists always believed in timber-framed, low-span, glass-houses orientated north/south to give plants maximum daylight. Because of the problems

Calceolaria forthergilli grown in the alpine house on open slatted benching.

associated with decaying wood, alumium has now become a popular material for glasshouse structures. Unfortunately, condensation problems with aluminium are far greater than with wood, which also tends to maintain more even temperatures and be slightly warmer overall.

With the advent of louvres, it is more practical to increase the surface area of ventilation than in traditional rod-operated ventilation systems as seen in the older alpine houses. During the summer months full ventilation should be provided to maintain cool conditions and in some instances this may mean doubling, or quadrupling, the original area of ventilation provided, depending on the greenhouse size, since smaller houses tend to be inadequately ventilated. In addition, the door is normally left open during the summer but covered with a fine mesh to prevent birds and, in some instances, other forms of wildlife either damaging the plants or pollinating the flowers of certain alpines.

Full ventilation may also be provided during the winter months where mild spells prevail. However, bearing in mind that in the wild many alpines are covered by snow and generally do not suffer extreme cold conditions, certain species will benefit from a little gentle heat, merely to prevent root balls freezing, whilst others will tolerate the relatively low temperatures experienced in the cold greenhouse. Always avoid warm conditions in spring which can bring plants into soft growth earlier in the season than normal, leading to uncharacteristic development and other problems.

The watering of alpines during the winter months is most critical. More plants are killed by the watering can than by any other cause. To some extent, these problems can be alleviated by the careful arrangement of plants in suitable containers on appropriate staging. Over the years enthusiasts have developed deep staging, often of iron or steel, but more recently in aluminium, with elaborate, sometimes ingenious methods of controlling the watering. Plants may either be directly grown in gritty compost over a layer of free-draining sharp gravel, or in pots sunk up to the rims into sharp sand. The sand around each pot, normally of clay, is then watered sparingly, allowing the compost to soak up small amounts through the pot.

On the other hand, many alpines can be grown very successfully on open staging with the plants housed either in clay or plastic pots. In some instances, a hybrid method of sinking a smaller pot within a larger pot and filling the gap with sharp sand can be employed; this is particularly effective with primulas and cyclamen. The open-slatted staging allows free and effective air circulation around the plants. However, pot-grown alpines in these conditions will require more frequent watering than those grown in a plunged or directly planted bed.

The large-scale alpine house at the Royal Botanic Gardens, Edinburgh.

One method of watering pot-grown alpines is to use a series of level trays or pans containing about 1½ in of water. Alpines grown in the same height of pot are stood together in the pans until sufficient water has been taken up by each individual pot; the amount will depend on the time of year and the plant in question. Plants are then placed where they may drain freely before being replaced on the open bench.

Second to over-watering, over-potting is a major cause of plant losses and repotting should only take place when absolutely necessary. Should the need arise, potting should be carried out in spring, preferably after flowering, and extreme care paid to watering for the first few weeks. Directions for composts are given in Chapter 17.

The third cause of plant losses in the alpine house can be attributed to pests and, occasionally diseases. But with today's safe preventative insecticides and fungicides it is possible to set up a spray programme to anticipate infection, rather than wait until the pest is seen and attempt to control it. There are a number of successful systemic fungicides and insecticides on the market and these are explained further in Chapter 18, together with information on the major pests such as red spider mite, vine weevil and slugs.

The range of plants that can be grown in the alpine house is considerable, but there can be no greater joy than seeing an extension to the normal flowering season with, for instance, crocus and cyclamen. These can provide all-the-year round colour and, in some instances, very pleasant scents. A number of books have been written on the more difficult alpine house plants but it is surprising how many easy-to-grow alpines can be accommodated. My list would include a number of early-flowering Kabschia saxifrages such as S. × *Elizabethae* and S. *burseriana*. The primula family contains gems such as P. × *bileckii* and P. × *auricula*, whilst a number of small narcissi provide a succession of colour from February until late April. Lewisias can be grown easily in pots, as can some of the hardy calceolarias such as C. *darwinii*. There are several members of the Ericaceae family, notably *Gaultheria* and *Cassiope*, that will grow and flower well in the greenhouse provided lime-free water is available.

15. Combining Alpine Features

One of the joys of collecting alpines is to combine many of the features already discussed to create a true alpine garden.

The successful application of this principle, on a large scale, can be seen in the Edinburgh Royal Botanic Garden. The alpine features include a natural rock garden of several acres, complete with stream, the water of which falls gently to form pools before draining away to the large pond below the Herbarium. A scree has been carefully constructed on the southern edge, almost as if a bursting dam had spread its stony mixture of rocks and plant debris where tiny mats of alpine nestle; and alpine lawns on either side are broken by outcrops of rocks that shelter other small alpine plants. To the east the rocks give way to an alpine area which blends into a moorland heather garden. To the west, peat walls, wild and woodland gardens provide a home for many shade-loving plants. The overall effect of this careful planning is most pleasing, and there is no reason why, with patience and imagination, it should not be emulated on a smaller scale in the average garden.

My second garden gradually evolved from a vegetable plot to an area combining peat walls,

some 40 ft long and 6-8 ft deep, facing north, a formal rock garden with sunny south-facing bake beds ideal for sun-loving alpines and dwarf tulips, together with a scree garden and a moist north-facing damp bank. Three small pools led down to a deep but confined water garden feature which with its constantly recirculated running water provided a welcome retreat from radios and electric lawnmowers.

A 6×8 ft greenhouse provided space for a mist propagation unit, a growing-on area, and home for a considerable collection of show auriculas. Alpine auriculas and a large collection of primulas were housed in dutch light frames which, when necessary, could be turned into an extension of the mist propagation unit. Around the garden twenty or more stone troughs, of varying sizes, accommodated the small gems. In anticipation of moving house, a quick count revealed about 1,300 different plants growing in an area of only 24×42 ft and this even included sufficient grass to sunbathe.

Having achieved such variety on a site measuring a mere 110 square yards, I am convinced that alpine gardening is suited to all gardens, regardless of size. Provided aspect, soil type, etc. are taken into account, a combination of many or all of these features can produce a fascinating all-year-round display. Indeed, to encompass so many different spheres on one site is something that is only possible when gardening with alpines.

The author's own garden (24 × 42 ft) showing a successful combination of garden features.

16. THE ALPINE GARDENER'S DIARY

There is no true start and end to work in the alpine garden, but we might as well stick to the conventional diary and begin in January. Although weather conditions at this season often deter all but the most ardent enthusiasts, there is a considerable amount of constructional work to be done, not to mention inside and outdoor maintenance, and planning for the rest of the year.

January

Weather permitting, heavy construction work can take place, provided the ground is not frozen or extremely soft due to heavy rain or snow, in which case it is easier and more pleasant to work in drier, safer conditions later on. A number of common alpines such as primulas, erodiums, geraniums, lewisias, morisias and platycodons can all be propagated from root cuttings taken from plants during this month.

February

Construction needs to be completed as soon as possible in order to allow soil to settle before planting. As the sun gains a little strength, the first annual weeds often appear towards the end of the month and should be removed at the earliest opportunity because species such as the hairy bittercress can produce seed within weeks of germinating themselves. Keep an eye open for snow and storm damage.

February is often a month of cold, drying winds and extra protection may be advisable for evergreens, particularly those with soft foliage such as hebes. The first of the alpine seed becomes available in February from Alpine Societies and seed houses, and should be sown as quickly as possible. Some of the autumn-sown seed, having been exposed to frosts, will be ready for pricking out and potting up.

March

Construction, even in the north, should be completed by now, and in the south spring planting can commence towards the end of the month. Lay out plants carefully before planting and ensure that all plants are watered in and carefully labelled to avoid confusion. Continue weeding with a hand fork and gently firm in any plants lifted by frost. Remove protective covers in the drier areas but avoid condensation and drips where glass, perspex, etc. remain in place. Remove previous season's top growth of herbaceous alpines. Top dressings can be applied, according to soil type and aspect, every one to three years. In shady areas, a mixture of leaf mould, peat, forest bark or well-rotted compost can be used, whilst in open situations grit and leaf mould can form the basis of a top dressing, applied approximately 1 in thick. On poorer soils, an application of bonemeal can be spread at 1 oz per square yard. Begin to trim edges of lawns; in mild areas and seasons the first mowings can take place. At the first signs of growth, many alpines can be lifted and divided, especially herbaceous types such as astilbes and hostas. Continue with pricking out seedlings and potting on, avoiding high temperatures in the greenhouse or cold frames, which will lead to soft growth.

April

This is perhaps the busiest month, with planting in full swing. Weeds will be germinating rapidly and require teasing out with a hand fork, taking care to avoid damaging bulbs and late-emerging herbaceous plants such as *Roscoea* and *Rhodohypoxis*. Continue top-dressing, where necessary, with an appropriate mixture, after removing any remaining glass covers, etc. which should be safely stored for the coming autumn. Keep up with jobs in the alpine house, paying special attention to gradually increased watering, and, if need be, apply shading to prevent burning of plants. Gradually harden off early seedlings by placing in the cold frame. Remember to take the camera out and capture some of the brilliant colour provided by the early-flowering saxifrages and primulas, but watch out for slug attacks as the weather becomes warmer.

May

On the east coast of the country this can be a dry month and it may be necessary to water sinks and peat gardens, together with any areas of light sandy soils. As air temperatures rise, aphids build up rapidly in numbers, and appropriate sprays should be used against greenfly, blackfly and whitefly. Soil-borne pests are also on the increase, and granular insecticides or soil drenches can be used against the larvae of the lettuce aphid and the immature vine weevil. May is the month of colour in the alpine garden and it is well worth visiting gardens such as Edinburgh's Royal Botanic Garden, Wisley and Ness Botanic Garden near Liverpool. In the north there is still time to plant out alpine beds, provided irrigation is available. Toward the end of the month the first seeds will be ripe and ready for collecting in paper envelopes which should be carefully labelled and stored in a cool, dry place.

June

Keeping up with the weeds and watering are the two priorities and it is also time to start pruning and propagating. Depending on locality, *Arabis*, *Aubrieta* and *Helianthemum* will have finished flowering and can be pruned hard to promote vigorous new growth which will carry next year's flowers. Newly planted alpines should be kept well watered, thoroughly soaking the ground to encourage deep root formation. Water in the evening for best results. Continue to collect and packet seed, and start to take softwood cuttings, with and without heels, according to variety. *Azalea* and *Syringa* can be taken as butter-soft cuttings.

while all others should be allowed to firm up but not become hard.

July

Alpine meadows which were ablaze with bulbs earlier in the year will now be ready for their first cut once the foliage of the bulbs has died down. The more vigorous mat-forming alpines may require pruning to keep their overall size under control and prevent invasion of more choice plants. Keep an eye on watering and pest and disease control, especially red spider mite, which rapidly builds up in dry weather. Continue seed collecting and take cuttings of any subjects when the material is in a suitable condition. Visit alpine gardens and alpine nurseries to get ideas and find those rare plants.

August

This is very often a wet month in many areas and an ideal time for killing the weeds in lawns, but take care that there is no drift or leaking of dangerous chemicals into alpine beds. August is ideal for taking evergreen cuttings and is the latest time for the majority of softwood cuttings. Alpine bulbs will become available towards the end of the month and the autumn crocus, together with *Colchicum*, should be planted as soon as possible. Continue to prune and restrain the more vigorous alpines, especially after flowering. Put down slug control where necessary.

Trim the cutting beneath a leaf joint.
NB The cutting will be 1-2 in in length.

September

Traditionally, this is the month to start rock garden construction or redevelopment, lifting and heeling-in plants where necessary and disposing of unwanted plants that have already been propagated. Remove shading from greenhouses and cold frames, and gradually reduce watering of these areas. Some planting of late-flowering alpines can be carried out during this month but in colder regions this is best delayed until late spring. Check over all alpine beds, planting bulbs, pruning to prevent wind damage, removing unwanted plants, and checking that those remaining are clearly labelled. Up-date planting plans and notebooks.

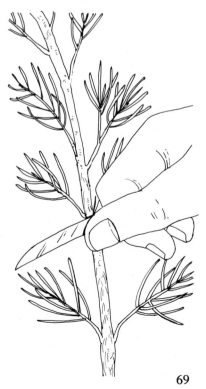

October

Continue with construction, getting large rocks on to the site before the weather breaks, cover alpine ponds with nets to prevent leaves de-oxygenating the pond, collect fallen leaves at the earliest opportunity and control slugs that thrive under these damp, wet conditions. Place covers over choice plants such as Asiatic primulas, *Meconopsis* and cushion alpines to prevent damage from wet conditions. Sow alpine seeds.

November

A good month for construction, with a hint of warmth still in the air, and a time for removing leaves almost daily from alpine beds and peat walls. Some mulching, if considered necessary, can be done at this time. Check the garden over in anticipation of the winter gales, ensuring covers are firmly fixed and that fences, cold frames, etc. will not be blown about. Order alpine seeds as soon as possible, lift and divide herbaceous plants. Plant bare-rooted trees while the ground is still warm.

December

This can still be a good month for construction in mild areas. It is a time to move indoors and mould alpine troughs, clean and packet seed, and sow a little of those which benefit from exposure to frost before germinating. The alpine house will need careful ventilation to ensure dry air is maintained. Bring planting plans up to date, ordering plants for spring delivery and making new labels. Check the garden over regularly for remaining leaves, fallen branches, etc.

Collecting leaves by using netting supported over the peat wall.

17. PROPAGATING ALPINES

Some people are good growers, some exhibitors and others propagators; but for any gardener there can be no greater joy than persuading seeds to germinate or cuttings to root, and in the alpine world, where cuttings and plants are so much smaller, it is even more fascinating. Due to the diversity of the plant range, there are innumerable ways of propagating alpines. As with all other forms of gardening, there are no hard and fast rules, merely observations; and if a particular method of propagation is successful, long may it continue. Some of these methods were included in a marvellous book entitled *Propagation of Alpines* by Hill (now out of print) and extending to several hundred pages; so in one short chapter it is only possible to introduce briefly some of the more common methods of propagation.

Seed is probably the most popular, but its source is important. As a rule, seed collected from species will produce plants relatively true to the original; on the other hand, hybrids do not always readily produce seed and, where available, can be extremely variable in viability and results. Home-saved seed can be sown while still fresh, with good germination results. Alpine Societies offer extensive seed lists, often running into several thousands of different species, and members are able to obtain these for only a few pence per packet. However, the inevitable delay in sowing will make germination more difficult.

Seed can be sown in trays or half-pots and covered, with twice as deep a layer of compost. Loam-based seed composts with added grit are preferred by many growers who use techniques such

Sowing alpine seeds. Scatter the seeds evenly over the surface of the soil.

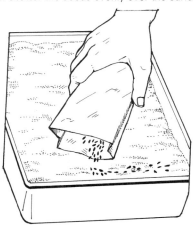

as covering with coal dust or grit and then placing containers outside for nature to take its course.

My technique is to store seed in polythene bags inside a refrigerator, sow at the earliest opportunity, and place out of doors during the winter months. Plants requiring a higher temperature to germinate are kept in the refrigerator until February, when they are sown and placed in a cool greenhouse. If no germination has occurred within 6-10 weeks they are placed in a polythene bag and put back in the refrigerator for a further 6-10 weeks (emulating the progression of summer and winter); often, on the return to the greenhouse, many seeds will germinate. If not, either repeat the operation or place in a cold frame or sheltered spot, and leave nature to her devices, as sometimes germination may not take place for several years.

Primula seed should always be sown immediately it is collected, as should *Meconopsis*; and in both cases germinated seedlings should be overwintered in a cold frame prior to growing on in protected beds until the following autumn. In most other instances, seedlings can be pricked off into well-drained pots of compost and grown under cool conditions until sufficiently large to plant out during normal planting seasons.

Impatience is normally the major reason for failure when raising plants from seed, but it is always worth considering the following:

Was the seed viable in the first place?

Have I sown it in a suitable manner?
Is it in a suitable environment to expect germination?
Has the seed rotted?
Despite germination, have the young seedlings died?

The answers to these questions and many others are covered in one of the TV Garden fact sheets, but if nothing seems to work, it may be helpful to consult plant collectors' books and notes to find out the conditions in which the plant grows and produces seeds and seedlings in the wild.

There are many other ways, apart from seed, of propagating alpines, and very often the success rate depends on using a suitable method at the correct time of year, according to the plant in question. The degree of skill and the equipment available, may, in some instances, determine which method of vegetative propagation is chosen. Let us look first at the simplest methods that require little or no equipment.

Division

This can be carried out in early spring or autumn on a wide range of subjects. Where plants are lifted with a fork or hand fork, the soil should be gently shaken or washed off to make division easier. As a rule, it is best to disregard the older centre part of herbaceous alpines, such as *Aster alpinus*, and the rhizome-forming iris, as they will have lost their vigour. Plants can be teased apart by hand or with a hand fork, but avoid using sharp instruments such as a knife or spade except for separating

mist propagation unit.

nked growing points, as in the
ase of the iris. Plants may be
eplanted immediately at the
ame depth and carefully
belled. Where autumn planting
s carried out, firming may be
ecessary after frosts; alternati-
ely, plants can be overwintered
n pots in a sheltered position.
stilbes, hostas and many multi-
emmed herbaceous plants can
e increased safely and cheaply
y this method.

rish Cuttings

his is a slight variation on division, suitable for plants whose
branches or stems, when in
contact with moist soil, form
roots. Dwarf cotoneasters and
the miniature willows, for
example, will root as they creep,
and generally it is best to lift
carefully rooted sections in
spring or early autumn and
either replant directly where
required, or pot up into suitable containers to nurse along
in a cold greenhouse or cold
frame until well established for
planting the following spring or
autumn. Some purists regard

this as cheating, but for many it is a method that requires little skill and gives a high success rate.

Cuttings

It is impossible here to describe in great detail the different methods of taking cuttings. Briefly, however, the season begins in late spring when small, very soft cuttings can be taken. As the season progresses, the cuttings should be slightly longer and the stem will become more woody. Since it is difficult to say exactly when a particular variety of plant will have suitable propagation material, it is best to practice what I term 'bracketing', i.e. taking several batches of cuttings over a 4-6 week period in the expectation that at least one batch will root well. The location, age of the plant and particular season will all affect the quality and availability of cutting material, and I have noted with interest that in some years certain varieties will root well in mid June, and in other years, late July.

In the majority of instances, non-flowering shoots are selected, and these are best collected during dull weather and kept in polythene bags prior to trimming. A very sharp knife or razor blade should be used to trim cuttings, usually beneath a leaf joint, as this is the point where the hormones can rapidly encourage callusing and subsequent rooting. Always prepare cuttings in a cool, shady place, and work ideally on moistened newspaper or damp capillary matting, as this reduces transpi-

Dip the base of the cutting into a proprietary hormone rooting liquid. (Rooting liquid usually comes in small containers.)

ration or wilting of cuttings. As a rule, the lower leaves are removed to prevent rotting when inserted in the cutting compost; however, there are a few cases where leaves are left intact. When cuttings are taken from large-leaved plants, such as *Hydrangea* 'Pia', I have found it best to reduce the leaf area of cuttings by half, using a sharp knife across the leaf. In any event, it is always worth taking a few experimental cuttings by various methods, as, for example, gently tearing a heel of older wood from the plant.

The cutting compost should consist of peat and grit, and ingredients such as perlite may be added to give improved drain-

Use a dibber to prepare holes for the cuttings.

...ge, aeration and warmth. The ratio of ingredients can be based on two parts peat, one part sand and up to 30% perlite, all by volume. Ingredients should always be clean, well mixed and moist, no fertiliser being required at this stage. I find it best to use either quarter seed trays or 3½ in square pots for the cuttings. The moist compost should be levelled off with the rim of the container and lightly firmed, using a presser board, which is simply a piece of timber the exact shape of the container, conveniently fitted with a handle.

With softwood cuttings it is best to use a piece of thin stick or a dibber to prepare holes which,

as a general guide, should be one-third the length of the cutting. A 3½ in pot will take nine or even sixteen cuttings, depending on size. Hormone rooting powders, in some instances, do seem beneficial but in others, such as *Phlox douglasii*, I have noted a marked reduction in rooting. Dip the base of the cutting into the liquid or powder and shake off any excess before inserting into the pre-formed holes. When propagating saxifrages and other small cuttings, such as *Armeria*, I find it best to fill three-quarters of the pot with cutting compost, top off with sharp sand and insert the cuttings into the sand, which appears to assist rooting. Cuttings should then be watered from above with a fine rose on the watering can to settle the surrounding compost.

Cuttings can be placed in a simple cold frame in a shaded corner of the garden or in a better lit position and covered with shading which can be removed during dull weather. Alternatively, they can be set in a more sophisticated propagation unit in the greenhouse or indoors. A closed case or unheated propagator, if placed in a warm position, can often provide the required humidity to encourage the cuttings to root. Occasional misting of the cuttings and shading during bright, sunny periods is often sufficient to promote rooting.

If a heated propagator is used, it should have an integral thermostat which will cut off the heat supply at a predetermined temperature; for alpines 68°F (20°C) is normally adequate. One word of warning, however; even with the heating supply off, the temperature under the plastic domes of these propagators can climb above 100°F (38°C), which rapidly kills cuttings, so that shading or ventilation will be necessary to avoid this. Where large-scale propagation is required, use can be made of mist propagation units, comprising a series of soil-warming cables buried in sand and connected to a variable thermostat to provide gentle bottom heat and thus aid rooting. But if all this sounds too sophisticated, take heart. A polythene bag placed over a pot of cuttings, held in place with a rubber band and kept in a north-facing window, can be surprisingly successful. Many of the easier alpine varieties can be rooted in this way.

Most cuttings will root quickly but any decaying leaves or cuttings that rot off should be removed at the earliest opportunity. Once rooted, cuttings should be hardened off ready for potting. A 2¾ in square pot is ideal for the purpose. Place a little grit in the bottom for extra drainage prior to potting, using a J. I. No. 1 with 25% extra grit. After potting, place in a cold greenhouse or cold frame in

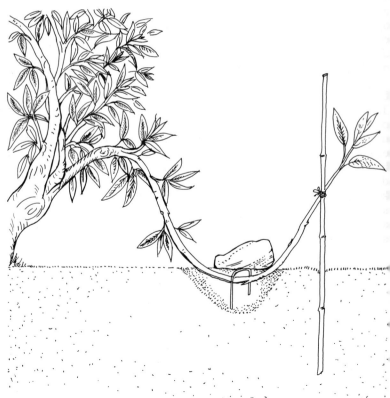

slight shade and grow on, watering as necessary, before planting out the following spring.

Other methods of propagation include root cuttings, which can be taken from sections of root lifted carefully from plants such as *Primula denticulata* and *Pulsatilla vulgaris*, in January and February. Cuttings are prepared by using sections of root 1-1½ in long, with a top cut at right angles to the stem, and a slicing cut at the bottom, thus ensuring that the cuttings are inserted the correct way up in the cutting compost. The pots are then kept in a cool or cold greenhouse until the shoots emerge from the sections of root, which are barely covered with compost. Avoid over-watering and do not be in a rush to repot as top growth is often in advance of root development, due to the warmth.

Layering

This is another simple method of propagating alpines which are more difficult than most plants to establish from cuttings. The low branches of plants such as rhododendrons are wounded with a knife, pressed into slight depres- · sions in the soil around the plant, and kept in place with bent sections of wire such as coat hangers. The soil is then replaced and a stone can be set over the pegged-down section to conserve moisture and hold the stem in position. The upper section of the branch should be tied to an adjacent cane so that it remains vertical. This is a slow method of propagation, best carried out in spring, and layers can normally be severed from the parent plant some twelve months later for replanting the following autumn.

Never be in a rush to plant out newly propagated plants; it is best to grow on all plants slowly to avoid soft, sappy, weak growth. Freshly potted plants should be kept in a shady position within a cool greenhouse or cold frame until established. I find plants are best overwintered in a cold frame with some variation even during the coldest weather. Watering should be reduced in the autumn and plants kept on the dry side until growth commences in early spring. Frame lights can be opened a little further as the temperature increases to avoid soft, leggy growth while at the same time watering may be stepped up. This provides good-quality hardy plants for planting out in April or May.

(Opposite) Layering: the wounded branch is pressed into the surrounding soil and secured with a bent piece of wire, which is then covered with soil and held in place with a stone. The branch is kept vertical by tying it to a cane. When the layer has formed new roots, it can be severed from the parent plant.

18. ALPINES IN TROUBLE

Rather than give this section the conventional title 'Pests and Diseases', I prefer to look at the difficulties encountered by alpines, including environmental problems and mismanagement. Compared with many other plants, alpines are relatively free from pests and diseases. Even so, regular inspection and correct interpretation of symptoms, whatever the cause, are essential preconditions for healthy, trouble-free plants.

It is always advisable initially to check and rule out environmental and nutritional imbalances, together with symptoms of over-watering, under-watering, etc. If all plants in the area appear to suffer from the same symptoms, the problem may be environmental, and appropriate action should be taken.

Powdery mildews often produce a white, felt-like coating on foliage and leaves of *Helianthemum*, *Clematis*, *Myosotis* and *Veronica*. Fortunately, they are easily controlled by the use of sulphur dusts or Benomyl.

Downy mildews are more difficult to control, as they live within the leaves of plants such as *Meconopsis*, *Primula* and *Alyssum*, only producing a white felty appearance as the fruiting bodies are formed towards the end of the season. Bordeaux mixture or Zineb applied to suspect plants early in the season may help to prevent infection.

Under warm, humid conditions a number of plants succumb to botrytis rot, first signs being a greyish white mould on soft tissues, followed by a soft wet rot penetrating stems and more woody areas, until the whole plant may be killed. Applications of Benlate or Supercarb give good control.

Rusts and smuts can attack a number of alpines. *Campanula turbinata* may be affected by the same rust as attacks groundsel. Violas, gentians, *Dianthus*, *Soldanella* and *Vinca* can all be attacked by various forms of *Puccinia* rust, for which there is no real control. The general rule here is to improve hygiene and reduce humidity.

Anemones, *Colchicum* and certain other bulbs occasionally produce foliage with raised black lesions. These are normally smuts which, when in an advanced state, rupture the tissue, spreading spores to healthy plants. The answer is to burn all infected tissue as plants cannot recover from these diseases.

Various viruses can be spread by leaf-sucking insects such as aphids. Delphiniums, for instance, can be stunted by cucumber mosaic virus, daphne produce twisted mottled foliage, *Arabis* is occasionally affected by ring spot, and violas may be affected by colour breaks. Some of the dwarf irises, such as *I. pumila* and *I. tuberosa*, can be affected by the iris mosaic virus, causing streaking and dwarfing of foliage.

Basal stem rots can occur in a number of plants such as campanulas, iris and violas, and in most instances a soft white rot sets in after a white mycelium has attacked previously healthy roots. Little can be done to save plants. Infected plants should be removed and the ground sterilised with a fumigant.

Armillariella is a serious fungal disease that attacks woody plants, travelling underground by black threads which explain its common name of 'bootlace fungus'. Armillatox will give relatively good control in certain circumstances, and where losses do occur all roots and stumps should be removed.

Forsythia and *Daphne* occasionally produce flattened or elongated stems due to a physiological disorder known as fasciation. There is no control and all infected parts should be removed and burnt.

The foliage of various alpines is occasionally infested by the frothy cuckoo spit produced by the larvae of the common green froghopper. High-pressure spraying with an insecticide will normally dislodge the froth and expose the larvae to the chemical.

Woolly aphid, which attacks a wide range of shrubby material, is often seen on *Cotoneaster* and *Ribes*. Its presence is signalled by white masses resembling cotton wool which contain either woolly aphid or mealy bugs, both of which are protected by a waxy substance, so that chemical control is difficult. In isolated instances, the use of cotton wool buds dipped in white spirit will burn out pests; or in cases of widespread infestation, the addition of a spreader to a high-pressure application of a suitable insecticide will, after several treatments, control the pest.

Several forms of scale insect may be seen on *Cotoneaster, Escallonia, Daphne*, etc. which are rapidly infected with sooty moulds feeding on the honeydew secreted by the insect. Control, where necessary, should be based on petroleum sprays or tar oil in the winter.

Primulas, cyclamen and fuchsias are often affected by the larvae of the vine weevil, which is rapidly becoming a pest of major importance. The creamy white grubs, approximately ¼ in long, eat the roots of many plants, while the adults will chew scalloped holes out of rhododendron and primula foliage. Gamma HCH may be added to potting composts as a deterrent, while lightly infected plants may be watered with Hexyl, a combined insecticide and fungicide, which has some control over larvae.

Several small green caterpillars will quickly devour the foliage of a wide range of alpines, especially primulas. The problem is normally caused by the caterpillars of the *Tortrix* moth family. Fortunately they are rather host specific, but where infestations occur, leaves should either be picked off and burnt, or a high-pressure contact insecticidal spray applied.

Ants, though causing no direct damage to plants, are rather annoying as they disturb the hair roots of many plants such as *Dianthus* during their excavations. Dust based on gamma HCH or pyrethrum seem more effective than traditional antkillers.

Worms may invade pots in cold frames and cause havoc, particularly among cushion plants and mat saxifrages. Lawn wormkillers seem to give good control.

Slugs and snails can be major pests in the alpine garden. The keeled slug, which spends the greater part of its life in the soil, is especially difficult to control. Slug pellets, whilst efficient on the larger surface-habit slugs, can cause problems with pets and the wildlife chain. Fortunately, products such as Fertosan have been thoroughly tested and result in non-toxic dead slugs. Nobble, an old formula recently revived, is used in low concentrations as a form of birth control to destroy future generations of slugs.

Red spider mite is a difficult pest to see, let alone eradicate. The symptoms are often mistaken for a plant that is merely struggling. Foliage turns rusty, is hard in texture and often shows a fine webbing on the underside. It takes a magnifying glass to see the small mites within the web which protects them from insecticides. Special red spider mite sprays, known as acaricides, are available to control certain stages of the life cycle and it is therefore necessary to repeat applications several times.

Greenfly can quickly build up on many alpines during warm

weather, but they do not cause serious plant losses. Where necessary, several applications of insecticides will break the chain of reproduction. However, as with whitefly, aphids build up a resistance to a particular chemical, so ring the changes regularly and always spray the underside of the leaves and young shoots.

Earwigs often devour young flower buds and distorted flowers are usually a sign of this early morning visitor. Traditionally, earwig traps made of upturned flower pots filled with straw or dried grass and placed on short canes give good results. Pots are either tapped over a bucket of water and the insects drowned, or the contents removed and burnt.

Mice love bulbs, especially crocus and cyclamen; and the damage is done underground, usually during the colder months, the problem tends to go unnoticed until the bulbs fail to emerge. A number of very efficient and safe traps are now available on the market but perhaps the best answer comes from an alpine nurseryman who regularly starves the cat and then places him in the bulb frame to let nature take her course!

Birds, particularly blackbirds, can cause havoc with mat plants when looking for nesting material or the soil-borne larvae of pests. Sparrows attracted by the colour of crocus flowers will quickly devastate early spring displays, apparently unnecessarily. A few strategically placed wreath wires from the local florist's shop will catch unsuspecting

A healthy *Colchicum* in August before foliage arises.

birds off balance, so setting off their own bird scarer.

Cats can be a great nuisance when defining their areas or territories, leaving large brown patches with an unpleasant smell. They may also be attracted by the scent of certain alpines. Suggested deterrents range from orange peel to holly leaves, carefully placed where the cats enter the garden. A new material called Cat Off joins a long line of cat repellents.

Dogs, foxes and other large animals appear to dislike the smell of fox oil or Renardine which is carefully brushed on strings suspended around alpine beds at nose height.

The above list may seem daunting but such occurrences, thankfully, are not all that common. The biggest pest is probably the ill-informed gardener who often does more damage than all the known pests and diseases put together.

19. LISTS OF ALPINES FOR SPECIFIC PLACES

It is difficult to prepare lists of plants for specific sites and with special attributes, when many are grown only in small numbers by a few nurserymen. So, rather than draw up a catalogue of numerous plants that are difficult to obtain, I describe in the following pages some of my favourite plants which have proved to thrive under certain conditions. The principle, however, remains unchanged. There are no hard and fast rules, and experiment is the name of the game.

PLANTS FOR THE ROCK GARDEN

Sunny pockets
Aethionema armenum – summer, flowering, pink 4 in.
Campanula cochlearifolia – June-Aug., blue, 4-6 in.
Dianthus gratianopolitanus – May-July, pink-red, up to 12 in.
Dianthus pavonius (syn. *D. neglectus*) – July-Aug., rose-red, up to 6 in.
Dryas octopetala – June, white, 4-6 in.
Morisia monanthos – March-May, golden-yellow, 6-12 in.
Onosma echioides – June onwards, pale yellow, 6-12 in.
Saponaria ocymoides – June, rose, 4-6 in.
Silvery saxifrages e.g. *Saxifraga burseriana* – summer, white, rose and yellow, 4 in.
Encrusted saxifrages e.g. *Saxifraga aizoon* – summer, white, rose, yellow and purple, 4-6 in.

Sunny joints
Androsace lanuginosa – June to Oct., pink with silvery foliage, 3-4 in.
Androsace sarmentosa (syn. *A. primuloides*) – May-June, rose with silvery foliage, 3-4 in.
Lewisia cotyledon hybrids 'Ashwood Strain' – Spring, white, pink and red, 2-9 in.
Saxifraga longifolia – June, white, 8-24 in.

Hot and dry situations in the rock garden
Mesembryanthemum varieties – June-July, red, pink, white, yellow and mauve, 2-3 in.
Sedum varieties – June-July, various colours, 1-6 in.
Sempervivum varieties – June, various colours, 2-12 in.

Carpeting plants
Acaena microphylla – summer, crimson, 1-2 in.

Arenaria balearica – March-Aug., white, 3 in.
Dryas octopetala – June, white, 4-6 in.
Hypericum reptans – autumn, yellow, 1 in.
Mazus reptans – summer, purplish blue, 1-2 in.
Saxifraga decipiens (syn. *S. rosacea*) and all mossy saxifrages –
spring, red, pink or white, 3-9 in.
Veronica repens – Sept., whitish, 4 in.

Cool damp pockets
Aquilegia glandulosa var *jucunda* – May-June, blue and white,
8-12 in.
Gentiana asclepiadea – July-Aug., azure blue, 6-24 in.

Cyclamen hederifolium.

Houstonia caerulea – June onwards, light blue and white, 3-6 in.
Hutchinsia alpina – May-July, white, 1-3 in.
Leiophyllum buxifolium – May, white and pink, 12-15 in.
Mazus reptans – summer, purplish blue, 1-2 in.
Meconopsis cambrica – June-Aug., yellow and orange, 9-15 in.
Primulas – various species and hybrids, spring and summer, 4-36 in.
Saxifraga umbrosa – early summer, pink, 12-18 in.
Saxifraga decipiens (syn. *S. rosacea*) and all mossy saxifrages – spring, red, pink or white, 3-9 in.

North-facing joints
Arenaria balearica – March-Aug., white, 3 in.
Haberlea rhodopensis – May-June, lavender blue with white throat, 4-5 in.
Primula edgeworthii – April, pale mauve with white eye, 4-8 in.
Ramonda myconi – May-June, purple, 4-8 in.
Saxifraga oppositifolia – early spring, purple, pink or red, 1-3 in.

Moist situations
Astilbe glabberima 'Saxosa' – late summer, pink, 4 in.
Cornus canadensis – white flowers in summer, then red fruits, 4 in.
Dodecatheon meadia – May-June, rose, 9-24 in.
Hosta venustata – one of several dwarf forms well suited to the rock garden.
Primula rosea – early spring, purple, pink or red, 1-3 in.
Primula japonica – May-June, purplish red, 18 in.
Primula pulverulenta – June, deep red, up to 3 ft.
Ranunculus alpestris – June-Aug., white with golden eye.
Salix reticulata – oval dark green leaves, 4 in.
Trollius europaeus – June-Aug., yellow, 1-2 ft.

Shrubs for the rock garden
Berberis × *stenophylla* 'Corollina Compacta' – evergreen yellow flowers April-May, only 15 in × 15 in after many years.
Buxus sempervirens 'Elegantissima' – small upright bush, white-tipped foliage, 4×2 ft.
Ceanothus prostratus – lavender blue flowers in spring, 6×3 ft.
Daphne × *burkwoodii* 'Somerset' – semi-evergreen with pink flowers May-June, 3×2 ft.
Forsythia viridissima 'Bronxensis' – yellow flowers in spring, true miniature, 12 in after many years.
Hebe buchananii 'Minor' – a slow-growing gem for trough and screes, white, 2 in.
Hydrangea 'Pia' – a *hortensis* sport with pink flowers in summer, 6 in × 6 in.

Dianthus 'Little Jock'.

Ilex aquifolium 'Hascombensis' – very slow-growing holly, 3 ft × 2 ft after 10 years.
Salix × boydii – tiny upright bush with grey leaves and silver catkins for trough or special spot in rock garden.
Sorbus reducta – a true miniature complete with pink berries in autumn, 18 in × 3 ft.

Plants for spring colour

Aethionema 'Warley Rose' – rich pink flowers over grey foliage in May, 6 in × 9 in.
Armeria caespitosa (syn. *A. juniperifolia*) – a Spanish thrift with almost stemless pink flowers, 2 in.
Aubrieta – various colours, ideal for walls and ground cover; prune after flowering
Bellis perennis 'Dresden China' – shell-pink flowers in spring, 2 in × 14 in.
Gentiana acaulis – huge, brilliant blue flowers, 3 in. Heavy soil, full sun, does not mind lime.
Phlox douglasii – various named forms of this tough, good all-round little plant.
Primula × pubescens hybrids – good free-flowering plants for full sun, 6 in × 6 in.
Pulsatilla vulgaris (syn. *Anemone pulsatilla*) – lavender flowers in April, full sun, 9 in × 9 in.
Saxifraga – Kabschia-type, flowers Feb.-April, full sun.
Saxifraga – mossy type, mostly vigorous mat-forming plants for moist partial shade.

Plants for summer colour

Acantholimon venustum – pink flowers above a mat of spiny foliage.
Achillea spp – sun lovers of various heights, with white or yellow flowers, gritty soils.
Aster alpinus 'Beechwood' – outstanding blue flowers on 9 in stems, any well drained soil.
Calceolaria fothergillii – for a gritty well-drained site, yellow flowers on 4 in stems.
Campanula cochlearifolia – 3 in stems support fairy bells of white or blue flowers.
Dianthus spp – many forms from 2 in to 12 in, in shades of pink, mauve, white, etc., lime lovers for a sunny site.
Erodium chamaedryoides 'Roseum' – small dark leaves and mats of white-veined pink flowers on short stems.
Hypericum olympicum – forms low bushes covered with rich golden yellow flowers.
Lithospermum diffusum (syn *Lithodora diffusa*) – for lime-free soil and full sun, named forms give brilliant blue flowers.
Thymus spp – mainly prostrate mats with tiny, often white or pink flowers that attract many insects.

Plants for autumn colour

Astilbe glaberrima 'Saxosa' – pale pink flowers in late summer, 4 in.
Cotoneaster congesta – creeping mound of foliage and stems, red berries, 2 in.
Cyclamen hederifolium – rose pink flowers in autumn, 2 in.
Gaultheria procumbens – white flowers followed by red holly-like berries, 6 in.
Gentiana × macaulayi – sky blue flowers from Aug. onwards, lime-free soil, 4 in.
Gentiana sino-ornata – azure blue flowers Aug. onwards, divide in April, 4 in.
Polygonum vacciniifolium – heather-like pink flowers, autumn tints to foliage, 3 in.
Saxifraga fortunei – white flowers on 12 in stems over bronze foliage.
Sedum spurium – carmine red flowers in Sept.-Oct., 4-6 in.
Solidago virgaurea brachystachys – a dwarf form of golden rod, late summer, 6 in.

Plants for winter colour

Chionodoxa gigantea alba – huge snow white flowers in Feb.-March, 4 in.
Chionodoxa luciliae 'Glory of the Snow' – violet-blue flowers with white eye, 4 in.
Crocus chrysanthus 'Blue Bird' – mauve-blue flowers edged white, orange centre, 3 in.
Crocus tomasinianus – lavender blue flowers in winter, ideal 3 in.
Cyclamen coum – shiny green leaves, flowers shades of red, pink or white from Christmas to March, 2 in.
Eranthis hyemalis – winter aconite, bright yellow flowers during mild spells, 3 in.
Galanthus elwesii – large flowered snowdrop from Turkey, Jan.-Feb, 6 in.
Hacquetia epipactis – yellow flowers before foliage in Feb., 5 in.
Iris danfordiae – vivid yellow flowers, Feb.-March, 4 in.
Iris histrioides 'Major' – large deep blue speckled flowers, Feb.-March, 3 in.

Plants tolerant of chalk or lime soils

Achillea	*Helianthemum*
Aethionema	*Hypericum*
Alyssum	*Iberis*
Anemone	*Leontopodium*
Armeria	*Phlox*
Dianthus	*Saxifraga*
Erodium	*Sempervivum*
Geranium	*Thymus*
Globularia	

Scree and moraine

Asperula suberosa – June-July, pink, 3 in.
Carlina acaulis – June, white, 12-18 in.
Dianthus alpinus – June-Aug., pink-red, 4 in.
Daphne petraea – May-June, rose, 3-6 in.
Draba bruniifolia – March, yellow, 4 in.
Leontopodium alpinum – June-July, enveloped woolly bracts, 6 in.
Lupinus ornatus – May-Oct., pinkish, 18-30 in.
Omphalodes luciliae – Summer, rose or blue, 3-6 in.
Oxalis adenophylla – May-July, lilac pink, 4-6 in.
Papaver alpinum – summer, white or yellow, 10 in.
Penstemon menziesii – June, violet blue, 1 ft.
Potentilla nitida – July-Aug., pink, 4 in.
Raoulia australis – mat-forming yellow plant.
Rhodohypoxis baurii – June-Sept., rose-red, 4 in.

Lewisia being raised commercially.

Moist lower end of moraine
Gentiana farreri – Aug., blue, 8 in.
Nierembergia repens – July, white and yellow, 2-3 in.
Saxifraga oppositifolia – early spring, purple, pink and red, 1-2 in.

Plants for covering sunny banks and dry walls
Alyssum saxatile – April-June, yellow, 12 in.
Arabis albida (syn. *A. caucasica*) – Jan.-May, white, 6-9 in.
Aubrieta deltoidea – April-May, lilac-red to purple, 6-9 in.
Campanula portenschlagiana (syn. *C. muralis*) – June-July, light blue, 6-9 in.
Cotoneaster microphyllus – white flowers, scarlet berries, slowly spreading.
Dianthus gratianopolitanus – May-July, pink-red, 1 ft.
Hélianthemum garden hybrids – June, various colours, 3-9 in.
Iberis sempervirens – spring and summer, white, 9-12 in.

Phlox subulata hybrids – April-May, rose-purple, 6 in.
Polygonum in var – late summer, heather-like red spikes, 4 in.
Thymus in var – the more spreading forms are best, various colours 3 in.

Plants for raised beds and dry stone walls
Artemisia schmidtiana 'Nana' – spreading mats of silvery foliage, 3 in.
Dianthus 'Little Jock' – pink flowers over grey foliage, 4 in.
Dryas octopetala – white flowers in summer over dark green foliage, 4 in.
Gypsophyla cerastioides – soft pink flowers over grey-purple foliage, 3 in.
Hypericum rhodoppeum – yellow flowers over soft grey hairy foliage, 5 in.
Penstemon pinifolius – orange-red tubular flowers, grass-like foliage, 6 in.
Sedum 'Rose Carpet' – glaucous foliage, rose-red flowers, late summer, 4 in.
Silene maritima 'Plena' – double white flowers over grey foliage, 3 in.
Thymus lanuginosus 'Hall's Variety' – purple flowers, hairy grey foliage, 2 in.
Veronica prostrata – dark blue flowers in early summer, 3 in.

Plants for alpine troughs and sinks
Alyssum serpyllifolium – prostrate mats of silver foliage, yellow flowers, 1 in.
Antennaria dioica 'Minima' – condensed form, 3 in stems with pink flowers.
Arabis ferdinandi-coburgii 'Variegata' – tiny variegated form, white flowers summer, insignificant.
Erodium chamaedryoides 'Bishop's Form' – large pink flowers all summer, 3 in.
Helichrysum milfordae – white flowers over silver mats of foliage in summer, 1 in.
Morisia monanthos – tiny tufts of foliage, minute yellow flowers all summer, 1 in.
Oxalis enneaphylla – white flowers over silvery folded leaves, 2 in.
Phlox douglasii in var – tough compact plants, covered in flower, early summer.
Primula × bilekii – pink flowers with white eye, early spring, 1 in.
Saxifraga 'Cranbourne' – blue-grey foliage, pink flowers in early spring, 2 in.
Silene acaulis 'Penduncalata' – almost stemless pink flowers all summer, 1 in.
Salix × boydii – grey-green leaves, cream catkins in spring, slow-growing, 12 in.

Dryas octopetala minor.

Alpine meadows
Camassia quamash – white-blue, 2-3 ft.
Crocus vernus – Feb.-April, white-purple, 3-4 in.
Crocus speciosus – Sept.-Oct., lilac, 4-5 in.
Geranium pratense – June-Sept., blue, 3-4 ft.
Gladiolus byzantinus – June, red, 2 ft.
Lilium martagon – June-July, purplish-red, 2-4 ft.
Lilium martagon album – June-July, white, 2-4 ft.
Narcissus bulbocodium – Feb.-May, yellow or white, 4-8 in.
Narcissus cyclamineus – Feb., lemon, 4 in.
Narcissus poeticus – April, white with red centre, 12 in.
Pulsatilla vulgaris – April, mauve or white, 8 in.
Saxifraga granulata – white, 12 in.
Thymus serpyllum (syn. *T. drucei*) – purplish, 1-3 in.
Tulipa sylvestris – April, yellow, 10 in.

Plants for paved areas
Acaena microphylla – rusty brown foliage and red burr-like flowers, 1 in.
Ajuga reptans 'Alba' – white splashes over grey green foliage, 3 in.
Antennaria dioica 'Minima' – tiny silver foliage and pink flowers, 2 in.

Dianthus deltoides var. – wide evergreen mats, red flowers in summer, 3 in.

Dryas octopetala – dark green leaves, white, yellow-centred flowers, 3 in.

Erinus alpinus – lavender flower spikes all summer, self-seeding, 3 in.

Helxine soleirolii – almost stemless green mats, any moist site, 1 in.

Mentha requienii – purple flowers over mats of tiny foliage, shady, 1 in.

Saxifraga mossy types – compact mats, red, pink or white flowers, 3-9 in.

Thymus serpyllum (syn. *T. drucei*) – creeping thymes, with red, pink or white flowers, 1-4 in.

Plants for the alpine house

Calceolaria fothergillii – red and yellow spotted flowers in spring, 4-6 in.

Convolvulus mauritanicus – blue, white-throated flowers in summer, 3 in.

Daphne petraea 'Grandiflora' – pink scented flowers May-June, 6 in.

Draba polytricha – dome of grey foliage, yellow flowers in spring, 4 in.

Hypericum trichocaulon – yellow flowers over evergreen foliage, summer, 2 in.

Paraquilegia grandiflora – lavender flowers, grey foliage, 2 in.

Primula edgeworthii – mauve flowers with yellow eye, 4 in.

Rhodohypoxis baurii – red, pink or white flowers all summer, 4 in.

Saxifraga grisebachii 'Wisley Variety' – rose pink flowers, spring, 12 in.

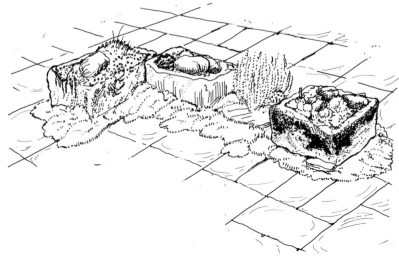

INDEX

The list of plants on pp. 56 and 82–92 are excluded from this index. *Italic* page numbers refer to illustrations.